Words of Life
Daily Devotional

A SEASON OF
CHANGE

Summer Edition

Stephanie M. White
Kathleen Higham

Contact the Authors:

We would love to hear from you!

STEPHANIE WHITE
**https://whitestephanie83.wixsite.com/
heavenonearthforyou**

KATHLEEN HIGHAM
kathleenhigham@yahoo.com

A Season of Change

Psalm 119:18,120 NIV
Open my eyes that I may see wonderful things in Your law. My soul is consumed with longing for Your laws at all times.

The Word of God is defined in Deuteronomy as our life. It is our very own Spiritual life.

This devotional is designed to take you through ninety days, the summer season, so that you can experience the change that only the Word of God can bring about.

Each season in the natural is marked by certain characteristics. As Christians, we will go through different seasons in our walk with God. Summer is a time when everything is in bloom, the air is fresh, and the sun is enjoyed. For farmers, summer is a time to plant *and* a time to harvest, depending on the crop. As a Christian, the Summer indicates a time of harvest and enjoyment, but it is also a time to continue planting the Seed of the Word. This devotional will provide you with that Seed to plant in your heart.

We trust that the Word will encourage you and it will produce Spiritual fruit in your life. Never take the Word for granted; praise God for it every day!

SUMMER TIME– by Stephanie White

Song of Solomon 2:10-12 NIV
My lover spoke and said to me, "Arise, My darling, My beautiful one, and come with Me. See! The winter is past; the rains are over and gone. Flowers appear on the earth; the season of singing has come…"

We are not meant to continually experience "winter." Trials are *part* of life, but they are not to be a believer's *way* of life.

It is possible for us to become comfortable in trials. We can begin to take root and pitch a tent in these tribulations if we are not careful. When we become accustomed to the trial, we are ignoring the promises of God. God does not keep us from trials, but He does provide for us so that we can arise out of them!

Our Lord is our Lover. No one's love can compare to His. His plans are based on His love for us. Trials are not designed to defeat us; His desire is for the trial to make us better. Arise! We are God's darlings! We are His beautiful ones! He calls out, "Come with Me!" Are we answering His invitation or are we too rooted in the trials?

Do you feel at home in tough times? If you do, then you must open the Word and gather up the promises of God. He has *good* plans for us! He wants us to arise out of the trials and take hold of His victory!

Is the Winter going on for what feels like forever in your life? If it is, then you must prepare for Winter to end. Abide in His promises of triumph and look ahead!

God is announcing the end of the Winter – can you hear Him? Take hold of His promise for new birth, new life, and an abundance of good! Open your Spiritual eyes and behold the flowers. Join with the birds in singing a new song – the song of Spring, the song of Summer, a song of praise to our God for His goodness! According to God you *are* blessed now! Winter is over! Take hold of the Summer of His Love!

Day 2
MATTER = WHO WE ARE - by Kathleen Higham

Who has the right to know the secrets written in our genomes? DNA, and now, what shall we do with all the complexity? Shall we map out 100,000 pairs of genes of 23 pairs of chromosomes, and read their entire sequence letter by letter? This would be a colossal task, for there are billions of letters; all the information required to make a human being is written into our data. The size of the matter is about a gigabyte of data. Your entire genome will easily fit on the hard drive in your desk top PC (paraphrased from National Geographic, "Secrets of the Gene," by James Shreeve -- Oct. 1999 issue)!

I am considering another matter of extraordinary data that I have stored in my laptop, my cell phone, and hold a hard copy in my hand. It is the Bible. Not in my life time will man breach the monumental boundaries of who we are. So then, who has the right to know and who shall we turn too with all of this complexity? Maybe on a cellular level man can marvel at the beginning and methodically and painstakingly search the complexity of life. Maybe science will graze the possibility of understanding this one gigabyte, but though science intrigues and mesmerizes in mindless awe; would one recognize who we are by what we saw? It seems man cannot believe his very own eyes. From the moment we are born, a miracle so incredible and astounding presents and yet some cannot believe even then— the miracle of life indescribably conceived, only to become inconceivable. Now we enter into a new world as "matter," because matter means to have mass and volume (occupy space). Here is another twist up the spiral staircase of our DNA; we matter to God! So, what then is the whole of the matter?

Not in my life time will science conquer the immensity of who we are. No! No one will break the code of the Creator. As scientists labor for the answers to life, the body is in a daily battle to die, but here is your hope: the Bible waits for you to seek the answer as you wonder why? You will find the unattainable is not about DNA, it is a Spiritual Matter, but the matter of our DNA is simply, God made us this way! However, our differences alone, because no one shares the same genome, will keep the genius moving from one cell to the next, finding himself constantly perplexed. I visualize the scientist rubbing tired eyes, as he looks into the microscope longing for the hope and dream of discovery. But, another path appears and on and on it goes, for in actuality, no one knows. Oh, the burden of the science amasses a heavy load, but not to our Father God, who designed the Creator Code! Yet here I write and wonder also. For the science will do good works and I will continue to ask the questions with no answers, as I feel my body slowly grinding to a halt. I wonder as if I were a scientist -- how, why, what, when? It seems this too has been incorporated into the DNA of men!

On a numerical note, there are roughly 3.5 billion letters in the human genome. If it were a book and you could read ten letters every second, it would take you eleven years to read aloud, not necessarily understanding what you read. There are roughly 3, 536,489 letters in the Bible. One might read the entire Bible in one year and in approximately 76 hours to simply read aloud, not necessarily understanding what you read. But, to study the Bible, a life time, I believe. I also believe the human code is the God code, no matter what the science may say! The God Code is the creation of life---that which we humans call DNA.

Lastly, I think it is rather interesting that our DNA is shaped like a twisted staircase. Some of us have been walking this twisted staircase trying desperately to reach the top, until we come to realize that the journey of life, though there will be twists and turns, if you continue walking upward knowing of the perilous curves, but none the less, we move upward, leaving behind that which we could not find. Full knowledge comes when we search for who we are in Christ and answer to His call. Up, up, up the staircase lies the Conclusion of the Whole Matter! Ecclesiastes 12:13 "Fear God and keep His Commandments, for this is man's all."

Have you ever wondered of this?
As you contemplate your own DNA
Can we grasp the sheer magnitude, or
Accept that God made us this way.

Oh, just the matter of conception
Seems simply impossible to believe
But yet the end result brings life
Your eyes cannot, will not deceive.

This matter, a substance that holds life
Speaks brilliance in such a way
That entices the genius to chase it
To understand the complexity of DNA.

Scientists will relentlessly pursue, then
From a drop of blood will expound
And when the answer comes to him
Does he know what he has found?

For this matter has absolutely no end
But the good works will surely endure
And life shall present as always
Then cling to the temporary cure.

The letter chain, a spiral staircase
Fascinates the intellectually curious
Yet life marches onward to death
This matter unchangingly mysterious.

Now this body was born to die, though
Natures allows some to grow old
Is it in the DNA? Perhaps
But Only God knows the Creator Code.

So, if matter explains who we are
Can man see what he saw? If so,
"Fear God, keep His commandments
For this is man's all."

My thoughts came from an article I read in National Geographic 12 years ago, and my endless well of numerical information from Wikipedia.

Day 3
KEEP YOUR FOCUS– by Stephanie White

Joshua 22:4-5 NIV
Now that the LORD your God has given your brothers rest as He promised, return to your homes in the land that Moses the servant of the LORD gave you on the other side of the Jordan. But be very careful to keep the commandment and the law that Moses the servant of the LORD gave you: to love the LORD your God, to walk in all His ways, to obey His commands, to hold fast to Him and to serve Him with all your heart and all your soul.

The tribe of Gad went back home after the Lord had given them rest. Once they returned home they decided to make their own altars instead of going up to the temple. We may ask, "What is so bad about that?" This was not simply a matter of avoiding a long journey to the temple; it was about doing things their way instead of God's way.

They were warned not to take their focus off of the Lord, but they did not listen. They were told to walk and obey. In the Hebrew these words mean to keep your focus on; hedge in your life; gather; take in and make part of who you are. Instead of keeping their focus on the Lord, they made their own altars and they drifted from the presence of the Lord -- which was represented by the temple. Today we drift from the presence of the Lord by staying out of the Word. We build our own altars -- like our family, our job, our finances, our entertainment, and the like. The very blessings that God gives us can keep us from Him if we are not convinced of our desperation for the Word of God. We decide to make things more important than God as a result of drifting from the Word. God knows that we have to put time into our families, our jobs, and so on, but God wants us to do these things through Him- He does not want these things to replace Him!

I SHALL NOT BE IDLE- by Kathleen Higham

Though not one to be idle
It seems a burden to rest
This mind God has busied so
Then enormously, He blessed.

Though not one to be idle
Sometimes I wondered how
But God was my Counselor
And I shall not be idle now.

No, no, I shall not be idle
When all is said and done
Work is the essence of my soul
His peace lifts the rising sun.

Though not one to be idle
There were many seeds to sow
Knowledge breathed life in me
Having studied just to know.

Though not one to be idle
So I taught those I bore
To work hard, work hard!
Then work just a little more.

Though not one to be idle
Age does not diminish my zest
I am still on this journey
Maybe someday I will rest.

Still, I shall not be idle
When God calls my name
Oh, I shall not be idle!
For He taught me the same.

Dear ones, I shall not be idle
But if my heart should roam
Then I will run to Him, when
He comes to take me home.

Proverbs 31:27
"She looks well to the ways of her household, and eats
not, the bread of idleness."

John 4:23 AMP
A time will come, however, indeed it is already here, when the true (genuine) worshipers will worship the Father in spirit and in truth; for the Father is seeking just such people as these as His worshipers.

What is a worshipper? By the original definition, a worshipper is someone who adores God. This means that a worshipper is passionate about God. They are stuck on God – they won't wander away from Him; they are abiding in Christ – for them to live is Christ. A worshipper is in love with God and we know that a person only loves Him *because* He first loved them (1 John 4:19); hence, a true worshipper knows that God is in love with them. They are intimately acquainted with His love.

A worshipper worships. What is worship? In Romans chapter twelve, verse one, we see the word "worship." This word is translated from a word that is defined as "ministration of God." What this means is that worship is Biblically defined as being cared for by God, supported by God, aided by God, assisted by God, and nurtured by God. God cares for, supports, aids, assists, and nurtures us because we are abiding in Him. Worship is a Spiritual action with a Spiritual source – God!

God is merciful; because of this, I can offer my body as a living sacrifice. "Offer" means "to stand beside" and it comes from a word that means "to abide." Offering has to do with counting on Christ / depending on Him / seeing yourself in Him. For us to offer our bodies is for us to abide in Christ and connect ourselves to Him.

True worshippers – those who are full of truth (the Word) – know that worship is Spiritual. THEY ARE GETTING THE CARE, SUPPORT, AID, ASSISTANCE, AND NURTURE OF GOD BECAUSE THEY ARE ABIDING IN THE WORD. They know that we cannot offer God worship – they know that worship is His gift to us! A true worshipper is consumed by God!

Day 6
GOD AND I- by Kathleen Higham

I am forever bound to God. Nothing can separate me from His love. No matter where I go, or what I do, my Savior watches over me from above. It was the miracle of His life and then His excruciating death on the Cross that brought to me salvation, eternal. In my soul His spirit brings a peaceful sigh. For every moment of my life, I shall never be alone. Why? Because He is with me always, God and I...

I stuttered and stammered
Breathed a peaceful sigh
For my Father God so loved me
He let His only Son die
Forever bound to Him
God and I.

How could this miracle happen?
To feel free and complete
For my Father God so loved me
As nails pierced His Son's feet
Forever bound to Him
God and I.

There is no condemnation
My sin was washed away
For my Father God so loved me
He gave everything on that day
Forever bound to Him
God and I.

Each morning as I pray
Words spoken in His name
For my Father God so loved me
Allowed Christ's suffering and shame
Forever bound to Him
God and I.

Another day shall surely pass
And all my fears will flee
For my Father God so loved me
He shared the Cross of Thee
Forever bound to Him
God and I.

Oh my Savior in Heaven!
Who sees the tears I cried
For my Father God so loved me
When to this life I died
Forever bound to Him
God and I.

Romans 8:38
**"For I am persuaded that neither death nor life, nor
angels nor principalities nor powers, nor things present
nor things to come, nor height nor depth, nor any other
created thing, shall be able to separate us from the love of
God which is in Christ Jesus our Lord."**

Day 7
PERFECT- by Stephanie White

Revelation 3:2 AMP
Rouse yourselves and keep awake, and strengthen and invigorate what remains and is on the point of dying; for I have not found a thing that you have done [any work of yours] meeting the requirements of My God or perfect in His sight.

We really do need to wake up and realize what we are doing. Are we producing Spiritual fruit or are we producing dead fruit? This church in Revelation did many "works," but Jesus said that not one of them was Spiritual. This should make us sit up and take notice.

Their works *appeared* Spiritual, but appearances do not matter to God. God is concerned with the origin of our works – are they of the flesh or are they of the Spirit – that is what matters to God. God's requirement is faith. Our works must be done by faith; they must be the fruit of abiding in the Word.

Too many times we are far too concerned with how things *appear*. We can do so many things that *look* Spiritual to the naked eye; we can impress many with our outward show, but that is not what really matters.

We need to rouse ourselves – we need to open our eyes to the truth of the Word. The Word is clear when it proclaims that apart from Christ we can do nothing.

> John 15:5 AMP I am the Vine; you are the branches. Whoever lives in Me and I in him bears much (abundant) fruit. However, apart from Me [cut off from vital union with Me] you can do nothing.

If we want to produce fruit that has Spiritual value then we must learn to abide in the Word; we must live by every word that proceeds from the mouth of God. The Word is our Seed; the Word is our Spiritual source.

Every morning and every night to His promises I hold tight. No matter where my heart shall go—as the dawn sweetly opens up my eyes or the inky black of night should quietly close my weary eyes; He knows. Truth, His truth is left behind for me to touch, and I need Him, need Him, oh so much. Father God for Your peace and joy I pray. Night and Day...

Father God, for Your peace and joy I pray
When glistening drops of rain shall fall
But in a timely manner leaves behind its truth
We who live and breathe and need so much
To feel the blessed rain that passed this way
Father God, for Your peace and joy I pray.

Father God, for Your peace and joy I pray
When the sun appears bright and warm
But in a timely manner leaves behind its truth
We who live and breathe and need so much
To feel the blessed sun shine down a ray
Father God, for Your peace and joy I pray.

Father God, for Your peace and joy I pray
When the night shadows harkens to the dark
But in a timely manner leaves behind its truth
We who live and breathe and need so much
To feel the blessed night when down we lay
Father God, for Your peace and joy I pray.

Father God, for Your peace and joy I pray
When another morning steeps inside this heart
But in a timely manner leaves behind its truth
We who live and breathe and need so much
To feel the blessed morning then humbly say
Father God, for Your peace and joy I pray.

Father God, for Your peace and joy I pray
When the twilight ambles to a glorious day
But in a timely manner leaves behind its truth
We who live and breathe and need so much
To feel the blessed gifts of night and day
Father God, for Your peace and joy I pray.

Father God, for Your peace and joy I pray
When silence waits, lingers, then reaches down
But in a timely manner leaves behind its truth
We who live and breathe and need so much
To hear the blessed Father speak, "I heard you pray"
Now peace and joy abounds to us, night and day.

Isaiah 28:9-13
"Who is it He is trying to teach? To whom is He explaining His message? To children weaned from their milk, to those just taken from the breast? For it is: Do and do, do and do, rule on rule, rule on rule; a little here, a little there." Very well then, with foreign lips and strange tongues God will speak to this people, to whom He said, "This is the resting place, let the weary rest;" and, "This is the place of repose"-- but they would not listen. So then, the Word of the LORD to them will become: Do and do, do and do, rule on rule, rule on rule; a little here, a little there-- so that they will go and fall backward, be injured and snared and captured.

What is the Word to you? It is NOT meant to be rule on rule, do on do! Do not look at the Word this way! Do not explain it to others this way! See it the way God sees it -- as a resting place, a place of repose. Repose means to be refreshed and at rest; it means to put your feet up and relax. God's Word is not a place of stress—it is your place of resting in Christ. The Word is our Spiritual Seed – when we plant the Word in our hearts we can then rest in Him. We can rest and let the Word of God work in us and through us just like God promised it would. God will do what He promised to do – God's Word will produce faith and that faith will produce Spiritual fruit.

God's Word is defined as our life in Deuteronomy. It is life as God has it. If we want to take part in the Divine nature, we are going to have to abide in the Word incessantly.

If we look at the Word as rules and regulations, God tells us that we will go and fall backward. Backsliding is the result of seeing the Word as a rulebook. We fall into the enemy's trap when we look at the Word this way. The Word is not meant to be lived up to; it is designed to enable us!

How do *you* see the Word?

Day 10
REST- by Kathleen Higham

I am drawn to the depth of the sea. This time of year it seems to call to me. Peace, calm, quiet, rest, sweet serenity. In my dreams tears carry me to my one true friend. Who could this be that created such a gift as the sea? It is He...

There are places in the sea
That calls deep unto deep
Where nothing disturbs it
And peace is yours to keep.

I dream of this place
A place that will never wake
Not even a ripple stirs
Could it be heaven's lake?

Find it in your soul
An abyss without end
A sanctuary just for you
To seek your one true friend.

Oh, who is this true friend?
That waits in your depth
When down, down you fall
Through endless tears He wept.

Find it in your soul
As you search deep within
Serene, quiet, peace, rest
At last...Rest in Him.

Matthew 11:28
"Come to Me, all who are weary, and I will give you rest."

Hebrews 3:18 KJV
And to whom sware He that they should not enter into His rest, but to them that believed not?

Those who believe enter HIS rest - not those who doubt! Jesus wants to rid us of stress so He furnished us with what we need to be who He called us to be – His Word! We do not need to be stressed about being good enough, about sinning less, about being more like Christ, or about anything for that matter --- all we need to do is get into the Word He furnished for us because it is all that we need! We can get into the Word and be at ease. We can focus on Christ and rest assured because *He* will do what He has promised!

Let us look at this in the day-to-day. If I am struggling with lying I must realize that I cannot change myself; instead, I need to get into the Word and find as many verses as I can on lying. I then need to abide in these verses – I need to memorize them, meditate on them, write them out, and so on. I then need to be still and let God be God! I need to let Him do what He promised He would do in me. If I do lie, then I need to continue focusing on those verses because I have not yet produced living faith. Only living faith produces the Spiritual actions – not my stress, not my forced efforts, not even my begging God to change me. He already told me He gave me everything I need to produce Spiritual fruit. He furnished me with what was needed (2 Peter 1:3) - I simply need to use it!

Romans 8:32 NASB He who did not spare His own Son, but delivered Him up for us all, how will He not also with Him freely give us all things?

Christ does not expect you to do this on your own! HE provides you with everything you need! Take advantage of it! Remain in the Word of God and receive everything you need!

Day 12
TODAY- by Kathleen Higham

I have a completely different understanding of what today
actually means. Have you ever heard the saying, "Today is the
first day of the rest of your life?" Truer words were never spoken
for those who have asked Jesus Christ to come into their heart.
Today as I read, Hebrews 4:7—God set a certain time, calling it,
Today! Today, if you hear His voice, do NOT harden your heart!
My "Today" was in December of 2000. If you have not begun
your day with "Today" it is time to open up your heart, mind,
and soul to hear His voice—allow Him to make "Today" become
tomorrow and forever yours. Have you and Jesus met? Have you
had your "Today" yet? Oh how I pray that you would see that a
life with Christ is from "Today" and to all eternity!

What is Today to you?
Do you wait for tomorrow?
In wonder of this life
And time you might borrow?

What is Today to you?
Have you listened for His voice?
He longs to be your Father
But have you made the choice?

What is Today to you?
For tomorrow may never come
Because Today is what we have
Maybe not even that for some!

What is Today to you?
Have you and Jesus met?
For your Today is nothing
If you have not found Him yet.

What is Today to you?
I pray that you might see
Then at last invite Him in, share
Christ, from Today - to all eternity!

Day 13
FREEDOM- by Stephanie White

2 Corinthians 3:17 NIV
Now the Lord is the Spirit, and where the Spirit of the Lord is, there is freedom.

Real freedom can only be found in the Spirit. We cannot walk in true freedom outside of Christ.

True freedom is not being free to do whatever you want. True freedom is walking at liberty and ease in Christ. It is freedom from living in fear. It is living a life of confidence in Christ, not ourselves.

Where is the Spirit of the Lord? Jesus Christ told us that He would send the Holy Spirit to us and the Holy Spirit would live in us.

> John 14:16-17 NIV And I will ask the Father, and He will give you another Counselor to be with you forever-- the Spirit of truth...He lives with you and will be in you.

The Spirit of the Lord is in us and we walk in that Spirit when we connect with the Word of God. When we ignore the Word of God we forfeit the freedom that God provides.

> Romans 7:23-25a NIV But I see another law at work in the members of my body, waging war against the law of my mind and making me a prisoner of the law of sin at work within my members. What a wretched man I am! Who will rescue me from this body of death? Thanks be to God--through Jesus Christ our Lord!

When we ignore the Word of God we are prisoners of our flesh. We cannot overcome our flesh and escape its power without the Word of God. We are hopeless outside of Christ. We need Him to rescue us and He is the Word. Through the Word of God we will live a life of freedom.

ONE THING – by Kathleen Higham

Luke 10:41
**"You are worried about many things, but only one thing is
needed. We are one in Him and only He can walk sorrow
down the path that leads to joy. The one thing we cannot
live without is His Word."**

Greatness comes when down we fall
And we did nothing, nothing at all
Not one thing, no not one thing
Yet in our sorrow angels sing.

Music flows from His song above
A mighty voice speaks of joy and love.
"Never, never," I hear Him say
Shall I leave you, not for one day.

One thing that we know for sure
His love is forever true and pure
The words of others truth may bend
But God's Word, it can never end.

One thing, one thing we must give
Our life surrendered and we will live
Remember on the Cross, our King
He died for this, this one thing.

His Word, can you hear Him call?
Greatness comes when down we fall
This one thing I pray you heard
One thing only—Is His Word...

Day 15
TREE SHAKER– by Stephanie White

Isaiah 61:3 NIV
…to bestow on them a crown of beauty instead of ashes, the oil of gladness instead of mourning, and a garment of praise instead of a spirit of despair. They will be called oaks of righteousness, a planting of the LORD for the display of His splendor.

We are the Lord's planting! And He planted us so we can display His splendor!

> SPLENDOR: to gleam, embellish; to boast; also to explain (i.e. make clear) oneself; to shake a tree:-- beautify, boast self, glorify self, vaunt self.

We are His planting, His fruit, and we were meant to boast about who He is. He wants to vaunt or make His beauty known through us. He wants to explain to the world who He is through us.

Did you notice "shake a tree--beautify" is part of the definition? Did you wonder why? During storms trees shake and in the process the old dead leaves and rotten fruit are blown off -- that is what He wants to do to us! He wants to use the storms of life to shake the dead stuff (the fruit of the flesh) off of you. In doing so, He makes us more beautiful! Don't fight the storm! Let the storm do its perfect work in you.

It does not matter if you are in a year of drought or not, you can still display God's splendor. Some of the most beautiful displays of God's splendor happen when people are in the tough times. If you watch someone go through a trial trusting the Lord and full of God's grace, it is a thing of beauty; so, plant yourself by the water and stretch out your roots! Water yourself in the drought. Remember- Jesus is the living Water and He is the Word; let Him display His splendor in you! You are His planting!

So, I have been a little stuck in the shadows these past few weeks. This morning I was incredibly blessed with an untitled poem written by one of my favorite poets. Allow me to share with you four lines that inspired me to write.

Still, still with You, when the purple morning breaks
When the birds awake, and the shadows flee;
Fairer than morning, lovelier than daylight,
Dawns the sweet consciousness, I am with Thee.

-Harriet Beecher Stowe

To His Light

The sun sinks down, down
Shadows of night come round
Weary eyes flutter, close, close
Drift in the absence of sound.

A final prayer lifted to Him
As peace inspires sweet repose
Resting beneath His pinions
Till the rising sun returns, glows.

The morning opens her book
To He who is the Light
A soul yearns, again, again
To speak of Him, and write.

Stillness beckons to those, His
That seeks the Word to share
From darkness till the dawn
The Father God was there.

The sun sinks down, down
Shadows of night come round
But those who belong to Him
Know they are heaven bound.

Weary eyes flutter, close, close
Drift in the absence of sound
Wait, wait, He is soon to come
With all the saints He has found.

On the clouds, He walks
Never again shall light retreat
Higher, higher, lifted up to Him
Until at last we shall meet.

The morning opens her book
As we fly to heaven's door
Carried beneath His wings of love
To His Light, a shield and buckler
To His Light, Forevermore...

Psalm 91:4
"He shall cover you with His pinions, and under His wings you will find refuge; His faithfulness is a shield and buckler."

Day 17
CHOOSING TO IGNORE THE BLESSING– by Stephanie White

Psalm 106:24-25 AMP
Then they spurned and despised the pleasant and desirable land [Canaan]; they believed not His word [neither trusting in, relying on, nor holding to it]; but they murmured in their tents and hearkened not to the voice of the Lord.

This verse in Psalms is very interesting when you dig into the original meanings of some of the words. Spurning and despising mean to cast off or refuse. The Israelites did not live by faith; they refused the Word. Are you casting off or rejecting the promises of God because you refuse to abide in the Word? Galatians, chapter five and verse two, tells us that Christ is of no profit to us if we distrust Him. Only faith brings God's promises to pass; faith that comes from abiding in the Word (Romans 10:17)!

If we do not choose the Word of God we are rejecting His promises. It is time for God's children to dwell in the Word of God and find out just exactly what He has promised!

His covenant is His Word (1 Chron. 16:15) and we are to be mindful of it. Meditate on what is yours in the Word of God. Faith will make those promises a reality! Do not give up on ANY of the promises God has made in His Word; He is not a man that He should lie. He is not limited by circumstances; He can do the impossible! Remember that it does not matter if you are the only one who abides in the Word and believes!

Romans 3:3 AMP What if some did not believe and were without faith? Does their lack of faith and their faithlessness nullify and make ineffective and void the faithfulness of God and His fidelity [to His Word]? God forbid.

Do *you* believe that God has blessings for *you*?

Day 18
I DECIDED- by Kathleen Higham

I have found that there are some people that inspire me to write. We sat in a lovely restaurant enjoying the scenic view and great conversation. She tells me that she never had a desire to run. I tell her, "Maybe you didn't have anything to run away from." Oh, if it were anatomically possible, smoke would pour from her ears as those genius wheels are spinning. She is completely tuned in to my very simplistic reasoning. Well, from now on when I am with her I will take my notebook, because she always gives me something to write about. Thirty years ago I threw my pack of cigarettes into the waste basket and ran out the door. It was a Forrest Gump moment. It may have run through her mind to say, "Run, Kathy, run!" but this is what she said, "You decided." Yes, she nailed it. I decided to stop smoking and change my life as I knew it. I decided. Now that is a great title for a poem and of course I fully expected my God to write it.

Every day is a day of decisions, but your life will never be the same if you ask the Lord to help you, then pray everything in His name. I ran countless races hoping to challenge the best. I ran for the trophy and it seemed an honorable quest. But running away from God made my weary soul long for rest. And one day, I decided, as I toed the line with a runner's zest. A fire burned inside me, for I had asked Christ inside my heart and when the gun fired, the race of my life would start. From that day on I ran with Him, still many tears were cried. But never again would I run away, for my Father God was right by my side. Everyone runs from something, but only you can decide. The Savior waits for you with His arms open wide. I will always remember that day when I chose then abided. Praising that day Jesus ran to me---The day when I DECIDED...

Looking back to troubled times
When life was tattered and torn
Oppressive and overwhelming
As despair uncovered the morn.

Each day brought perplexity
Decisions that had to be made
There was no one to turn too
I felt so helplessly betrayed.

No direction seemed feasible
And the battle raged within
Destruction became my mantra
I ran long and hard with my sin.

But mercifully came the prelude
Introducing this life to come
So out the door to face it I went
Began my true mission to run.

Not sure exactly how I decided
Running frantically from my loss
Until I ran with abandonment
And decided to run to the Cross.

No longer would I run away
For the path became quite clear
Run, run, run to the Father
There is nothing left to fear.

At last I had finally decided
On this most amazing day
I was running to my Savior
Never again would I run away.

Running to His arms open wide
With a contrite heart, I confided
Confessed and repented of my sin
Praise the day! Praise the day!
I decided...

Hebrews 12:1
"Wherefore seeing we also are compassed about with so great a cloud of witnesses, let us lay aside every weight and the sin which does so easily beset us, and let us run with patience the race that is set before us."

THANKFUL– by Stephanie White

Proverbs 25:14 KJV
Whoso boasteth himself of a false gift [is like] clouds and wind without rain.

As we enjoy the promises of God we must never forget how we received them. The Bible tells us that faith and patience bring about the promises (Hebrews 6:12). We must never get to the point where we feel like we have earned or deserved the gifts that God has *given*.

We cannot boast of the things that God does in our lives. His blessings are not earned; they are received. When we feel like we deserve these gifts we fall into the trap of pride.

Pride is a fruit of the flesh. Pride creeps into our lives when we fall away from our desperation for the Word of God. When we realize how much we need the Word we will remain in the Word and the Word will produce Spiritual fruit in our lives and pride will be avoided.

Apart from Christ we can do nothing of Spiritual value, but we can do things that *appear* Spiritual on our own. These things that we accomplish in our flesh are only done in vain. God tells us that boasting in ourselves is useless – just like storm conditions without the rain. We need the rain to water the earth; the appearance of rain does not cultivate anything. It is the same with our works of the flesh. They may appear Spiritual but they are of no Spiritual value if they are not done by faith.

These works of the flesh can lead us into a false sense of accomplishment; we must be aware of this. When we begin to feel like we can boast about the things *we* do, we can then know that we need a refresher course on pride and humility. Open the Word and find out what God has to say about man's pride. Meditate on John 15:5 – apart from Him we can do nothing – nothing of Spiritual value. Our lives are to boast in God alone!

Day 20
HAVE YOU CONSIDERED MY PRAYER? - by Kathleen Higham

"Waiting is beautiful and patience is divine." This is a quote from Streams in the Desert. I can speak with absolute clarity acknowledging that waiting and patience have not been gifted to me. In actuality I have prayed for patience and waited impatiently to acquire these gifts. I am quite needy in that I must know why, when, where, and how much longer must I wait? My mind is surely inquisitive and in the matter of lacking patience along with the inability to wait, I have found a quiet place where the insanity of life is quelled by my Father God who opens up His hand to accept yet one more personal request. If He wasn't God, He would need a thousand angels to hold them. My eyes can visualize my prayers pouring from His fingertips and tumbling down, but I know that He is God and holds each and every prayer in His mighty hand. This morning I thanked Him first for all He has planned. Maybe someday I will understand, but for now I must wait patiently and see, until He comes and speaks to me, "Child come follow Me."

Hold this thought for it truly is wonderful and I love when the poetry syncs up with the devotional, but I procrastinated a few days and now there is more to ponder. I had a delightful experience in the bank a few days ago, but first allow me to digress back in time and share with you my thoughts on God and His perfect timing in regards to our prayer requests. When I was in nursing school I had a roommate that was very devout and often I would observe her reading the Bible. On one particular day most of us were studying throughout the night for a make it or break it exam on neurology. It was the most difficult final and many nursing students would not survive this test. So, we drank coffee and crammed until it was time to take the test. My roommate prayed, read her Bible, but did not study for the exam. I asked her if she would like to study and she told me that God would see her through. Well, God and my roommate packed up the next day and He saw her through the door and out of nursing. I never saw her again. How interesting that I thought about her and recognized that maybe I am following a similar path, because God so graciously gave a gift to me, a novel, but I have not done much promoting. Was I thinking He was going to do it for me? It is no big feat to ask God to consider our prayer request, but why is it so hard to prepare the way for His answer? Ok, we made out some fliers, I learned how to send out an event on facebook, and I emailed some of my local friends. I even spoke in church which everyone knows is not my gift. The problem is that I am just not a sales type person. I don't like to ask people for anything, but I went to my familiar bank and asked my friend if she would post a flier about my upcoming book signing. I gave her a copy of the book which she held in her hand for about a minute before I took it back from her and placed it in the hand of a lovely man. We made eye contact as I sat in the bank manager's office. This man is going places and God is running right beside him. It was my pleasure to meet and enjoy a few moments with our Mayor, Jay Williams. God has a way of encouraging us through those He places in our path. Mayor Williams blessed me and encouraged me to trust in God for His promise and His constant consideration of my prayer.

Morning calls as prayers abound, but
Sometimes I weary of what I see
Still He fails me never, whispers
"Child, come follow Me."

Oh how I long to follow Him
But I whisper back, "Life's unfair"
And I am so, so tired Lord
"Have You considered my prayer?"

Still He fails me not, whispers
"I have plans for you dear one"
I cry, "How long must I wait?"
He says, "Wait until I am done."

"Well Lord, I am already done
And it seems I cannot go on
Have You considered my prayer?
Lord, where have You gone?"

He indulges me in my weakness
Then He speaks encouragement
"I am always right beside you
Did you really believe I went?"

"No, no forgive me Father
I know that You are there
But I can't help but wonder
Have You considered my prayer?"

The softest breeze caresses me
In the warmth of His holy sigh
"I have considered your prayer
Someday you will understand why."

This morning I thanked Him first
For every moment He has planned
He has considered my every prayer
The promise He holds in His hand.

"All the Rivers of Your grace I claim,
Over every promise write my name."
(Streams in the Desert)

Romans 11:35 NIV
Who has ever given to God, that God should repay Him?
For from Him and through Him and to Him are all things.
To Him be the glory forever!

We must understand that God will never owe us a blessing. We can never do enough "good" deeds to deserve a promise. We actually cannot *do* anything for God; He is not served by human hands (Acts 17:25). Instead of trying to do *for* God, let us begin to receive *from* God.

Any Spiritual gift you have is FROM HIM, anything Spiritual you do is only done THROUGH HIM, and TO HIM goes ALL the glory, praise, thanks, and so on!

If we took delivery of what we *deserved* from God, we would be in trouble.

Isaiah 57:12 NIV I will expose YOUR righteousness and YOUR works, and they will not benefit you.

Nothing we can do on our own apart from Christ is profitable. Fortunately, God does not treat us the way we deserve to be treated - according to our works or actions. Isaiah 61:7 tells us that instead of the shame and disgrace we deserve, we receive a double portion because we belong to God. We receive an inheritance - something freely bestowed on us after a death (in this case, a death on a cross). We also receive everlasting joy and we are supposed to rejoice in what we have been given. God has given us blessing upon blessing that we do not deserve. We need to quit looking for what we deserve and we need to understand what has been freely given!

As God's children we need to take the focus off of earning and deserving and we need to be inheritance minded. Remember that instead of our disgrace we can rejoice in our inheritance from our God!

Day 22
YOU, YOU, YOU, AND YOU– by Kathleen Higham

Several years ago we went to the Mother's Day service taught by the late, Pastor David Verzilli. He was a lovely man and a marvelous teacher. He started by saying that he planned on talking about mothers, but God changed the teaching and Pastor David taught on depression. It was an incredible teaching and so this morning when I reached for my notebook I had hoped to write a devotional about mothers, but God changed the devotional.

Upon awakening, my initial thought was to thank God that I am still here. Then I pray to not fail Him within the next five minutes of this life He chose to prolong. Trust me dear friends, because it is not that difficult for my mind to wander away from thoughts of God.

Sometimes I get weary of proclamations from others about who will be going to heaven and why, and who will not be going to heaven and why. Maybe that is why I heard a knocking on my door today and there stood a woman and her daughter. The woman was breathtakingly beautiful and I knew immediately that she was a Jehovah Witness. Of course she wanted to share the Bible with me and I felt so tender toward this woman for the simple fact that she was willing to put feet to her faith. I told her that and gave her a book of poetry. She asked if she could hug me. There were tears in her eyes when she walked off my porch, yet we are miles apart in our Christian belief. I smiled as I set down the tract she gave to me. I watched her hug that book about our Lord and Savior to her heart. Now I need to get back to this business of who is going to go to heaven, I have a little trouble with people, sinners like me thinking they actually know the answer, no matter the cost! But whose cost was it really? Certainly not ours! The cost was thirty-three years: From Nazareth to Gethsemane to Calvary...The cost was the Cross! I am unable to find the Scripture that states: "I, God the Father of the Savior, Jesus Christ, appoint you, you, you, and you to know who will celebrate in jubilation with Me when the doors of heaven open wide. You, you, you, and you; can you actually see who is sitting by My side? I believe God's Word is an instruction manual to help us assemble our life. The parts may be scattered and beleaguered with strife, but step by step we may follow until we reach this place and then call on His Holy Name and receive His saving Grace. You can expect to miss a step or turn down a wrong road. There is no doubt you will slip and fall beneath a heavy load. And when at last you make it, the task is now complete, but you missed a part. A part unassembled lies at your feet. Well, life might work without that part, because everything looks right. So, you tuck away the part, not listening to the cry of your heart.

Success comes with much hard work. You are thankful to God, but a niggling doubt appears and it seems ridiculously odd. Each morning brings a new day as you look into the mirror. There's the thought again. You push it aside and softly whisper to yourself, "I have everything in my career. I have honor, respect, love, friends, health, money and power. This is amazing for me. So God what is it that You are asking, probing, and longing for me to see? I am running through life holding on to a few, but not one told me of the absolute joy they knew. I have everything! I do! But, recollection comes of the one tiny part I hide, instead of giving it to You. Oh Lord, search my heart and wash me of my iniquity and any wicked way You find. Search me oh Lord, for the part I left behind."

Only God knows who I am and the sin I could not claim, but I was saved that very moment I called upon His Holy Name. Now hear this; you, you, you, and you, I live my life in prayer, for every soul who left behind that part they couldn't share. If you confess with your mouth that Jesus Christ is Lord, and believe in your heart that God raised Him from the dead, well, I shall see you there when Jesus comes to call. So bring along that missing part, remembering: Jesus died for all...

That one is surely going to hell!
I have heard a brother say
It left me simply speechless
When one could speak that way.

How can we ever really know?
What is buried deep in a heart?
Only the Father can truly see
For He holds the missing part.

Oh, it is with relentless fervor
They quote furiously the Word
There is no question in their mind
It seems considerably absurd.

That one is surely going to hell!
Yet I see no sorrow or grief
They take you to the very page
Then point the finger of belief.

But I stumble here, wonder
What then is God for?
And why did He have to die?
If a sinner can close the door?

I long to ask the question
About that one going to hell
What if God and that one spoke?
But God decided not to tell.

Could there be a relationship?
Between that one and God?
Private whispered words of love
Surely one must not find this odd.

Some cannot, will not waiver
No matter what the cost
But God holds the missing part
Of the one thought to be lost.

You, you, you, and you
I am planning to see you there
So don't forget to bring along
That part you couldn't share.

Because, you cried out His Name
And He heard the sinner's call
For you, you, and yes, that one too
Christ died for one and for all.

Romans 10:9
If you confess with your mouth, "Jesus is Lord," and believe in your heart that God raised Him from the dead, you will be saved.

Romans 10:13
"Everyone who calls on the name of the Lord will be saved."

Day 23
NO THANKS NECESSARY– by Stephanie White

Luke 17:7-10

"Suppose one of you had a servant plowing or looking after the sheep. Would he say to the servant when he comes in from the field, 'Come along now and sit down to eat?' Would he not rather say, 'Prepare my supper, get yourself ready and wait on me while I eat and drink; after that you may eat and drink?' Would he thank the servant because he did what he was told to do? So you also, when you have done everything you were told to do, should say, 'We are unworthy servants; we have only done our duty.'"

Does God thank us for the things we are "told" to do? The meaning of the word "told" is "to thoroughly arrange." We are under obligation to produce Spiritual fruit because God thoroughly arranged for us to be able to produce Spiritual fruit by giving us His Spirit and His Word. It is our privilege to depend on Him for everything because we are useless or unprofitable without Him. It is our duty to abide in the Word.

> Ephesians 2:10 NIV For we are God's workmanship, created in Christ Jesus to do good works, which God prepared in advance for us to do.

> God does not owe us thanks or a blessing for what we do. When we do something Spiritual we need to thank *Him*! He thoroughly arranged for us to be able to do it. He is the One who prepared us to be able to do the good works by giving us of His nature. Only when we are acting in the nature that is HIS workmanship, the part of us that is created in Christ, are we enabled to do those good works!
> Why should He thank us or be pleased with us for something only He is responsible for? Apart from Christ we can do nothing of Spiritual value (John 15:5)!

Upper Room Ministries had a wonderful outreach dinner last Sunday. As I walked through the tables offering drinks and talking with those who came, I made eye contact with a woman about my age. She was sitting with her 90 year old mother and her sister. I sat down and talked with these lovely ladies for some time. The woman was a very sweet gal and I told her how blessed she was to have her mother with her. "Yes," she said. Then very softly she spoke as she leaned closer to me and said, "But I lost my son, my only son." Her eyes filled with tears as did mine and I responded, "There are no words." Her son died of a brain tumor ten years ago, but it seemed as if it was yesterday to her. My hand reached out and wiped a tear from her face. A total stranger stepped into that holy place where God resides and waits to shower her with peace and grace.

If you know me, then you know that I give my books away as God instructs. On this particular Sunday the book lying across from us on the table belonged to this woman. When I gave it to her she was baffled and asked me why I chose her. Well, it was because she shared with me the most intimate brokenness of her heart. "I have lost my son, my only son." She made me think of another woman who lost her Son on a bloody cross. In my lifetime I have learned that a mother can lose a son through physical death, emotional death, or spiritual death. Still my heart longed to speak of the promise of our Father God from His Word. Isaiah 44:3 "I will pour out My Spirit on your offspring, and My blessings on your descendents." Isaiah 59:21 "My Spirit, Who is on you, and My words that I have put in your mouth, or from the mouths of your children, or from the mouths of their descendents from this time on and forever." Isaiah 66:22 "As the new heavens and the new earth that I make will endure before Me," declares the Lord, "so will your name and descendents endure." This was most assuredly a Divine appointment. She tells me that everyone has their own private sorrow and I agree, but the question is: How do we live each day with the heartache? Do we place it at the foot of the cross? I am hoping and praying to see this woman again. I am hoping and praying to feel her peace. "I have lost my son, my only son," she said. No matter how the loss portrays itself, our Father in heaven is fully aware and understands. He gives us His Word and His promise for our children. He called us woman and gave us a son, but more importantly, He gave us His Son, His only Son. Today is the day for recognizing women and the incredible strength God instilled in them. The Father God choose a woman to be the mother of His Son, the only begotten Son. She would suffer the most unbearable pain of all, yet there is very little mention of her in God's Word.

Women have been given the gifts of strength, courage, compassion, and exhortation. We are born with the desire to lift each other up. I know just about every woman in this room and I can state with absolute clarity that each of you have suffered, lost loved ones, but here you are, still...willing and desiring to lift up those in need. This is what I call, "A Woman's Creed." Especially those who have lost a son; God is mindful of this one. Even on that desolate day when your heart simply cannot pray, He sends the Holy Spirit who moans and groans to intercede. God hears the silent cry and meets your every need. Women who have lost their son are the perpetuators of "A Woman's Creed." He works in you and through your son, in you His work is never done...

"There are no words," I said
Reaching out to wipe her tear
A stranger I had never met
Yet God would draw us near.

"I lost my son, my only son"
In her brokenness came a plead
We shared the intimacy of grief
And the heart of a woman's creed.

For only a mother can understand
The sorrow of the ultimate pain
A trial comes so unspeakable
As the fires pour down like rain.

"Oh my God," she cries out!
My son was everything that mattered
Now a heart beats cold and empty
Her world was completely shattered.

The sun may shine, not for her
Relentlessly, time passes even still
When a memory plagues her soul
Of a man dragging a cross up a hill.

"I lost my son, my only son"
In the despair of that night
But the mother of God before me
Knew, that agony brings the light.

The Son of God, the only Son
Who was crucified to fill our need
So a dark and void heart could speak
The words of a mother's creed.

"Oh my God," she cries out!
Your work in me is never done
To perpetuate forever, a woman's creed
For our Lord and Savior, the only Son.

Day 25
THE MEANING OF CONTENT- by Stephanie White

Philippians 4:11 NIV
...I have learned to be content whatever the circumstances.

Being content is not about settling.

CONTENT: satisfied, not settling. Happy, joyful.

If we want to be content we are going to have to remain in the Word. The Word makes us content. The Word enables us to be happy with our current circumstances without giving up on receiving God's promises in the future.

Contentment is being satisfied; it is not settling. Always remember God has big plans for you!

Jeremiah 29:11 NIV "For I know the plans I have for you," declares the LORD, "plans to prosper you and not to harm you, plans to give you hope and a future."

Psalm 40:5 NIV Many, O LORD my God, are the wonders You have done. The things You planned for us no one can recount to You; were I to speak and tell of them, they would be too many to declare.

God has so many awesome things in store for us! We need to live our lives continually expecting God's promises to come to pass; we need to expect more and more of God's blessings. When we live believing things will never get any better, we live a dreary life. Where is the excitement in that? How can we be passionate about a life that will never change? We need to see the future through God's Word! Do not say, "This is it - this is all that God has for me so I am just going to accept it." When we read the Word we see God has so much more for us. Expect more while enjoying where you are!

WAVES OF MERCY AT THE KINGDOM DOOR– by Kathleen Higham

Pray for each other in the Spirit. See the Kingdom Door open wide. Behind that door lies one lone tear, seeking all the tears we've cried. When thundering waves crash to the shore, you can feel His mighty power, but waves of mercy will follow the storm that came in your darkest hour.

One lone tear falls down, down, mingles with our own. He cries, utters prayers of intercession; in the waves, hear the sound of His moan.

When death comes so unexpectedly, waves crushing in despair, with racking pain that seems endless and impossible to bear---He is there...

But, we must pray for each other in the Spirit, as we never have before! For one lone tear, waves of mercy, will open wide the Kingdom Door. Pray for each other in the Spirit, as we never have before! Safe haven at the Kingdom Door and the life we are longing for:
Eternal Life with our Father God.
Eternal Life Forevermore...

Powerful, unexpected, mighty
Unspeakable pain left in its wake
Crushed by the storm, not destroyed
All things happen for His sake.

One lone tear poured down, down
The wave came, swept him away
The Kingdom Door swung open wide
When he met the Lord that day.

Waves of mercy lifted her
To the Heavenly Father on high
He touched her battered heart
Then caressed her with His sigh.
One lone tear poured down, down
Carried her back to this place

Surrounded by all who love her
And the strength of His grace.

Waves of mercy wash over her
Close her eyes in restful sleep
He cries softly to His daughter
No more tears shall you weep.

One lone tear poured down, down
Waves of mercy ebb and flow
Safe haven at the Kingdom Door
On that day only God could know.

Pray for each other in the Spirit
Cry out, as we never have before!
Waves of mercy and one lone tear
Brings eternal life forevermore...

Psalm 107:25-30
**"For He spoke and stirred up a tempest that lifted high
the waves. They mounted up to the heavens and went
down to the depths; in their peril their courage melted
away. They reeled and staggered like drunken men; they
were at their wit's end. Then they cried out to the Lord in
their trouble and He brought them out of their distress.
He stilled the storm to a whisper; they were glad when it
grew calm, and He guided them to their desired haven."**

FREEDOM- by Stephanie White

Galatians 3:13 AMP

CHRIST PURCHASED OUR FREEDOM [redeeming us] from the curse (doom) of the Law [and its condemnation] by [Himself] becoming a curse for us, for it is written [in the Scriptures], Cursed is everyone who hangs on a tree (is crucified).

Jesus purchased our freedom – He paid the price in full for our sin! God hates sin; sin had to be punished. Thanks to Jesus Christ we do not have to incur the punishment – Christ took the punishment for us and He fully met all the requirements necessary for the wages of our sin to be paid in full.

Romans 8:3-4 NIV For what the law was powerless to do in that it was weakened by the sinful nature, God did by sending His own Son in the likeness of sinful man to be a sin offering. And so He condemned sin in sinful man, in order that the righteous requirements of the law might be fully met in us, who do not live according to the sinful nature but according to the Spirit.

When we are dependent on Christ we are living "according to the Spirit." Living according to the Spirit is living according to the Word. The Word tells us that apart from Christ we can do nothing of Spiritual value – if we are living according to this truth then we are living dependent on Christ. We are living knowing that Christ met all the righteous requirements for us and we do not have to live as if we still need to pay a price for our sin!

If we are living according to the sinful nature (the flesh) then we live OUT of agreement with the Word and we try to pay the price for our sin. We live with the burden of our sin instead of living free from that burden!

Day 28
THE DOOR– by Kathleen Higham

Revelation 3:8
"I know your deeds; What He opens no one can shut, and
what He shuts no one can open. I know your deeds. See, I
have placed before you an open door that no one can
shut."

The Behind Closed Doors paintings by Kathleen Denis cry out to God to open the door of life and rescue the innocent victims of human trafficking and slavery. This horrific attack on women and children is portrayed on canvas by Kathleen as she opens the door to expose the horror. Her expressions in these incredible scenes come solely from God who moves her hand, then paints the cry for help.

Will you help Kathleen Denis in her ministry and hear the cries of those innocent victims, "Behind Closed Doors?"

Their innocence was stolen
And they wept in the night
A ravaged heart so broken
Not strong enough to fight.

There seems to be no answer
For the suffering of a child
They should have been protected
But instead they were defiled.

The offense is so heinous
Yet our Father holds them tight
He's with them until the end of time
They are perfect in His sight.

Lord, hear the cry of my heart!
As the canvas screams for more
To rescue these innocent victims
God, please open up the door.

I stand before you weeping
As my heart reveals the horrors
Knowing You can stop their pain
Crush the evil behind closed doors.

I believe, I believe in You
Your mighty hand will open wide
The door that no one can shut
Where a million tears were cried.

My brush may paint the story
But You have heard the scream
They run to You through that door
When at last You paint the scene.

God will come to rescue them
In Him their hearts shall soar
He opens the door no one can shut
They are with Him forevermore
No longer behind closed doors.

Day 29
ALL THINGS– by Stephanie White

Romans 8:32 NIV
He who did not spare His own Son, but gave Him up for us all--how will He not also, along with Him, graciously give us all things?

Do we honestly understand what God has done for us? He has given us His Son. He did not hold back; He made the ultimate gesture of love.

If God was willing to give up His Son, why do we doubt that He will do other things for us? We doubt many times because we are focused on ourselves. We must realize that God will bless us *through Christ*. We are now joint-heirs with Him because of what Christ has done for us.

Romans 8:17 NIV Now if we are children, then we are heirs--heirs of God and co-heirs with Christ, if indeed we share in His sufferings in order that we may also share in His glory.

We are children of God; we are joint-heirs with Jesus Christ. We see that sharing in His sufferings is part of being a joint-heir. What does this mean?

First, let us look at what *His* suffering is. When did Jesus suffer? He suffered in the garden when His Spirit did battle with His flesh (Luke 22:44). He suffered to the point of sweating drops of blood. As we engage in the battle of our Spirit versus our flesh we are then sharing in His sufferings.

This Spiritual battle finds its victory as we abide in the Word. God promises us victory; He promises us that we will share in Christ's glory.

We do not have to limit ourselves. Every promise that God has made is for us (2 Corinthians 1:20). In Christ we *are* blessed! Open the Word, abide in the Word, and look forward to receiving from the Word!

Remember the old saying, "Be careful what you wish/pray for? You just might get it." I used to think that the prayer would be answered exactly as you asked. If we prayed for patience then suddenly there would be this wonderful calm as patience settled into our heart. If we prayed for unselfishness we became immediately of the giving nature, generous to a fault. If we prayed for strength and humility, then courage comes powerfully, but with a submissive spirit. If we prayed for faith, then the Holy Spirit would fill us with everlasting joy and an absolute trust in God. If we prayed to be like Christ, then we would humbly fall down and accept the life of the Lamb. We become meek and mild, tender in all our ways. If we prayed for gentleness, the Spirit flows sweetly into us as we soften every word and action. If we prayed to love others, our faces glow and our hearts would long to embrace our brothers and sisters.
But, when we pray and ask our Father for patience, unselfishness, strength and humility, faith, to be like Christ, gentleness, and a desire to loves others, well, things happen...

I have prayed for patience over and over again. It is a relentless prayer because there seems to be no end to the demands from others. Often there is no patience to be found in me, but my God allows the test. He answered my request.

I have prayed for unselfishness only to find myself battling to meet the needs of others when I can't even meet my own needs. I struggled because I failed to simply let God meet my needs. We are born with perfect selfishness, in our very first breath we scream for immediate gratification.

I prayed for strength and humility, but I fell completely apart when I needed to be strong and lift up another. Instead I was the one lifted up. Oh, humility did come briefly when I realized my weakness. I cried out to God knowing, "When I am weak, He is strong."

I prayed for faith fully expecting God to empower me, but every heartbreaking circumstance rolled through my life. They were crushing, devastating blows that only God could carry me through. Faith comes when you acknowledge that on the other end of your pain is the hand of your Father reaching out to you.

I prayed to be like Christ then backed away from the lowness of life because it offended my delicate senses. There was a flash, a vision of the Cross. I wanted to be Christ-like, to give my life freely, to help others, to be as an innocent lamb. I prayed to be Christ-like in ignorance, yet I believe He smiled at my request.

I prayed for gentleness and my tongue spewed words and my heart became irritable in the moment of need. I am amazed for the one who truly cries out for that gentle touch. I long for that quiet peace, but the world bellows her pain. Unrest is all around me, but He remains beside me, still.

I prayed to love others. They came in droves. The most unlovable and aggravating people I have ever met. Now they grate on me, impossible to look at or be near, yet He embraced them and me, until my foolish heart would see—His unfailing love.

Be careful what you pray for. Things happen when you pray. You might not like it, but things happen anyway...

I prayed for patience
Please God hear my plead
Let me be Your servant
To meet another's need.

I prayed for unselfishness
For this I truly knew
I am ready for this gift
There's nothing I won't do.

I prayed for strength, humility
But did I pray it through?
Will these things happen to me?
God, how I wish I knew.

I prayed for faith
For God my heart will grow
With a longing to believe
Lord, please let it be so.

I prayed to be Christ-like
An unimaginable goal
Envisioning the Cross, the Lamb
Who lives inside my soul.

I prayed for gentleness
But words came harsh, cruel
Teach me how to wipe away
The tears of a broken soul.

I prayed to love others
But I had failed to see
I needed God most of all
So unfailingly, He came to me.

Be careful what you pray for
Things happen when you pray
Be careful what you pray for
You just might get your way.

Day 31
THE PRICE OF FREEDOM- by Stephanie White

Luke 4:18 NIV
The Spirit of the Lord is on Me, because He has anointed Me to preach good news to the poor. He has sent Me to proclaim freedom for the prisoners and recovery of sight for the blind, to release the oppressed...

Freedom isn't free – but it is paid for! Jesus Christ came to set us free; He came to release us! *He* was the price that needed to be paid.

FREEDOM: pardon, deliverance, forgiveness, liberty.

We have been pardoned thanks to Jesus Christ and the price He paid with His life. God sent Him to proclaim this message to us and He is still proclaiming it to this day through His Word. Are we listening?

Galatians 5:1 NIV It is for freedom that Christ has set us free. Stand firm, then, and do not let yourselves be burdened again by a yoke of slavery.

Jesus Christ did not give His life to set you free just so you could continue to live a life of bondage! Christ set you free so that you could LIVE in freedom! Are you, or are you living a life of bondage? We can live in bondage to others, their opinions, sin, wrong thoughts, and the list goes on. Anything that burdens us is something we are in bondage to. Since Jesus died to set us free, let's enjoy it!

God is proclaiming your freedom! He is proclaiming it repeatedly in His Word. You are the only one who can choose to take hold of the Word, abide in the Word, and enjoy His freedom. We no longer have to live in bondage. We no longer have to live a life where freedom is evasive. Today is your day of freedom! Today is your day to begin living in the Word.

We are all capable of skirting the edge of insanity. It is a dark, cold, empty void of nothingness.

My heart does not have one smooth, unblemished spot on it. It is scarred beyond recognition, yet it pounds and thrives and seeks life. My heart longs to feel God. Only His hands that created me and produced the first electrical impulse that began my existence can heal the scars that map my heart.

It might seem like a handicap, but in actuality scarring toughens to some degree. Scarring is healing in that the open defenseless wound becomes layered with a protective covering. A scarred heart has great potential if it does not become a hardened heart.

Have you checked your heart lately? There is a certain amount of scarring on every heart, but some have more than others. A heart that never felt this battle may not make the best foot soldier for God.

Battle scars are reminders of the fight. My friend Stephanie wrote a book called, "Faith is Worth Fighting For." And I believe this to be true. So, we are in a battle, we have acquired the scars from the fight and now it is time to guard our heart and stand firm. We must remain armored in Christ, for He has designed the human heart to beat for all eternity with Him.

Can you remember your very first scar? When was the exact moment when a perfect little heart felt the pain that only another human being could inflict?

I was in a very affluent grade school. My dad was a truck driver. We lived from paycheck to paycheck. I did not fit anywhere in this school, yet my heart longed to have friends. When I was in sixth grade a sweet girl actually invited me to her birthday party. Her name was Kathy Fish and I will never forget this precious girl. I went to the party, but felt very much out of place. Those early school years were so hurtful and it seemed that every day I would come home with a stomach ache. One morning I sat behind a boy that was tormented unmercifully by some of the other kids. He came from a poor family. He looked disheveled and his dress was somewhat slovenly. He was obese and possibly a little slow. I cannot speak for sure about his capabilities because in retrospect, he must have been extremely guarded. We had a teacher who was a strong disciplinarian. She was downright scary. She would walk up and down the rows of desks with a ruler in her hand and strike out at anyone who was not paying attention. Sometimes I would day dream in class. On one particular day I saw her barreling towards me with her ruler raised. I closed my eyes waiting for her to strike me. Unbelievably she stopped in front of me and began what seemed to be the most vicious attack on that poor boy that I sat behind. I kept my head down as she screamed at him and called him a lazy, stupid boy. She hit him repeatedly with that ruler and demanded that he tuck in his shirt. I remember feeling the horror of it, but at the same time I was grateful that it was not me that she was attacking. This was my first heart scar and I have carried it inside of me for all these years. That was the beginning of my understanding of pain that comes when people hurt each other. I still think of that boy and I wonder if he survived the heart scars of his life. That same teacher grabbed me by my shirt and jerked me hard when I stepped out of the lunch line. She tore my blouse and humiliated me, but not one of us kids would ever tell our parents about her. In those days if you were reprimanded by a teacher, you were in double trouble if Mom and Dad found out. Obviously this is not the case today. Well, in fairness I must tell you that there were other teachers who were loving and kind. Sister Marie was an absolute dear. She encouraged me to write. Writing was the one area of my life where I could shine and this wonderful woman spent a lot of time polishing my tiny scarred heart. Of course writing was lost in the shuffle when I began to search for my career. So, here I am writing about my first heart scar. My family was so loving. We were poor, but I can say with clarity that I never experienced a heart scar from my parents. It seems my first heart scar was for the suffering and horrific humiliation of another human being. Maybe, just maybe that was the impetus for my desire to become a nurse.

Heart scars have come in various trials throughout my life. God has blessed me with a sturdy heart. My eyes have witnessed the brutality of mental illness. These pitiful souls are not only scarred, but often they are shattered. They travel a burdensome road that leads to the darkest void, but there is hope. God can and will light their way. There were some days when vacant eyes would stare back at me as they walked in despair. A heart would pump life into them and they waited for one person to care. Oh, let me tell you that I have seen those who cared. I have worked beside the doctors, the practitioners, the nurses and staff who truly cared.

Hearts may have been scarred and shattered, but there was always hope.

I wonder about Edward. His name was Edward. The boy who sat in front of me in grade school remains a remnant of an old scar. Edward surely had a scarred heart too, but no one will ever be as scarred as Jesus Christ. So, I believe that Edward has been blessed by the Lord, because, well, the Lord found it in His beautiful heart to bless me...

"I blessed you," He said
"I know it," I cried
Over fifty years gone by
But the memory burns inside.

A tender heart was battered
Recalling those hurtful years
It has surfaced for a reason
To think of it brings tears.

What good can come of this?
To retrace each step of pain
Well, it embraced my career
To help those thought, insane.

"I blessed you," He said
"I know it," I cried
Hearts scarred and shattered
Renewed when Christ died.

Renewed, restored and rescued
"I blessed you," He said
A scarred heart hopes, because
"I blessed you," He said.

Psalm 119:45 AMP
And I will walk at liberty and at ease, for I have sought and inquired for [and desperately required] Your precepts.

Walking or living in freedom is the result of making the Word of God your MOST DESPERATE NECESSITY. The Word of God leads you into a life that is free! Bondage has no access into a person's life when the Word is preeminent.

Seeking the Word means you are frequently in the Word; you seek the Word because you are a worshipper – you live your everyday life through Christ (Romans 12:1).

You inquire for the Word; you ask for more of it in your life. You ask God to fill you with His Word. You desperately require it; you refuse to live without it. You do whatever you have to do in order to get as much of the Word in your life as possible – you listen to the Word on CD, you read the Word, you think about the Word, and so on. The Word cannot be on the backburner in your life if you want to live a life of freedom!

We can walk at liberty and we can walk at ease. Ease is defined as effortless. Living at ease is living dependent on Christ instead of on our own efforts. We no longer place the burden on ourselves; we abide in the Word and we depend on God's promises. God's Word tells us that His Word will not come back void (Isaiah 55:11). When we are living at ease it is because we understand this verse. We know that we cannot change ourselves, but we also know that He can. We know that the Word will produce faith in us and we know that faith will produce Spiritual fruit. Instead of trusting in our efforts, we trust in God alone.

We can live a life that is carefree. We do not have to worry, live under stress, or be burdened. We can live at ease – we can live trusting in the Lord and all that He has done for us when the Word is our top priority.

THE PORTRAIT– by Kathleen Higham

God paints the picture of my life
Who I am, created by His hand
It seems years have come to pass
And every stroke was surely planned.

But still, I wonder who I am
The portrait unfinished, maybe so
Colors bright will make me smile
Dark and faded colors bring me low.

God paints the picture of my life
Every day an unexpected change
Only He knows who I am
His brush will always rearrange.

When will He add the final touch?
Time is flying faster and faster
A Holy Hand holds the brush
The Artist is my faithful Master.

Now at last, the work complete
The portrait done for all to see
His hand created who I am
With unfailing love He painted me.

PROCLAIM FREEDOM- by Stephanie White

Jeremiah 34:17 NIV
Therefore, this is what the LORD says: You have not obeyed Me; you have not proclaimed freedom for your fellow countrymen. So I now proclaim "freedom" for you, declares the LORD--freedom to fall by the sword, plague and famine. I will make you abhorrent to all the kingdoms of the earth.

Are we proclaiming freedom or are we encouraging bondage? Too many times we encourage bondage!

How do we encourage bondage? When we promote fear we are encouraging bondage. Any time we suggest that we need to be afraid of God we are bringing people into bondage if they do not know better. Too many people use fear as a method to thwart sin. God's Word never tells us that fear will promote Spiritual behavior – only faith will, and faith is the opposite of fear! Fear is of the flesh and fear keeps people in bondage.

People also encourage bondage when they put other people down. People who live in fear of rejection are imprisoned by what other people say about them. We should never speak negatively about others. Set them free from your opinions by seeing them according to who they are in Christ.

Bondage is encouraged when we suggest that we must live by the law. The Word clearly tells us that attempting to live by the law curses us (Galatians 3:10)! We are to be led by the Spirit, not oppressed by rules and regulations.

The list of ways we can keep others in bondage can go on and on. If we do not understand the freedom that we have in Christ we will not be able to encourage others to live freely. The verse above says that they did not "obey" God. This word means to take the Word in and make it part of who you are. Abiding in the Word keeps us out of bondage and it brings us into God's glorious freedom and we can share that with others!

Day 36
NOW- by Kathleen Higham

Today is my Father's birthday. I am thinking about the time we shared together. Of course the time is long passed and I find peace in knowing where he is, but I miss him. I don't know why God didn't allow me to have more time with my Father, but I was surely blessed by the time we did share. My Father was a loving, thoughtful, generous man. He had a sense of humor that was famous! If you ever met my Dad, you can be sure he would make you laugh. I pray to have some of his good gifts. Someday time will not burden and it makes me so glad, as my heart follows the sound of his laughter; I am in the Now with my Dad...

We cannot think apart from time
Because we are living in it
We cannot know what lies ahead
If sorrow weighs us down to quit.

We cannot think apart from time
Only God knows the beginning and end
Step out in faith and walk with Him
Don't fret what's around the bend.

We cannot think apart from time
Or envision what the future will hold
Just trust in God for everything
Be strong in the Lord, be bold.

We cannot think apart from time
God so understands our hesitation
So down He came, died for us
Making time for a personal relation.

We cannot think apart from time
When perfection will make us free
Then we will walk with our Father
Where time will no longer be.

We cannot think apart from time
Until we see around that bend
Discovering that time is endless
But time can be our friend.

We cannot think apart from time
Don't question what God will allow
With Him there is no past or future
For in Heaven there is only the Now.

Day 37
THE LICENSE TO SIN LIE EXPOSED– by Stephanie White

Romans 6:14-18 NIV
For sin shall not be your master, because you are not under law, but under grace. What then? Shall we sin because we are not under law but under grace? By no means...But thanks be to God that, though you used to be slaves to sin, you wholeheartedly obeyed the form of teaching to which you were entrusted. You have been set free from sin and have become slaves to righteousness.

The "license to sin" theory is just that – a theory! A theory is pure speculation. It is not a truth based on the Word and if you are abiding in the Word you know this theory is totally flawed.

If we are abiding in the Word our desire to sin will diminish. YOU CANNOT LIVE IN THE WORD AND IN SIN AT THE SAME TIME – IT IS IMPOSSIBLE! The Word enables you to walk in your Spiritual identity.

> Galatians 5:16 AMP But I say, walk and live [habitually] in the [Holy] Spirit [responsive to and controlled and guided by the Spirit]; then you will certainly not gratify the cravings and desires of the flesh (of human nature without God).

Walking and living in the Spirit is walking and living in the Word habitually. Jesus told us that His Word is Spirit (John 6:63) and when we abide in the Word we will NOT be manipulated by our flesh; our Spirit will have control. It is the ABSENCE of the Word in our lives that gives our flesh the right-of-way. Living under "grace" is living under the influence of God and God never influences His children to sin; therefore, any person claiming the license to sin is clearly NOT under the influence of God!

When I was a young woman I would see parents at the mall and their toddlers were tethered to them with a harness and a leash. It seemed extreme to me. Now there is this invisible, but spiritual correlation to the Christian family that tethers their child to Christ.

Children miss so much sin. What? Aren't we all born into the world sinners? Yes. We certainly are, but children can miss sin. If they are brought up in a Christian home where God is the head of the house, I truly believe children will miss much sin. We never have to teach them as babies to be demanding, or to have temper tantrums, but as they grow and witness the Holy Spirit of God in the family, they veer away from sin. Sin will always be there, yet the Christian family will focus their eyes on Jesus, bringing that child along with them. Children miss so much sin when families are tethered to God. A child may stray ahead and walk into the sin, but many will turn back to that place where they have been. It is instilled in them a sense of righteousness, for we know not one of us will leave this world alive. The children of God belong to the family that will survive. Survive to a life and promise of eternal bliss. Oh praise God to belong to such a family as this. And thank You Lord for all the sin the precious child shall miss. Some might wander a bit, when worldly freedom calls. They might. But when life stretches the tether tight, the longing comes to do what is right. Children can miss so much sin. It is a precursor for the young that readies them for the fight. The fight for a Godly life will always be. But, God will speak to those who wish to hear and see. "Miss the sin, miss the sin dear child," He says.
"For you are tethered to Me."

Children will run to everything
Not knowing to be afraid
Straying to the danger zone
Leaving parents feeling dismayed.

Our God is so encompassing
When families invite him in
A spiritual life will tether them
And the children will miss the sin.

It's true; we are all born to sin
For the world is filled with strife
But when Jesus is your anchor
You belong to the Christian life.

There is a soulful longing
That desires to do what's right
Christian families that follow God
Are strengthened for the fight.

The world wants to take us
Then draw us into the sin
Praise the Lord, our Savior God
Who holds us close to Him.

Children of God turn around
To hear His Word and see
"Miss the sin, miss the sin"
For you are tethered to Me.

John 15:1-2 KJV
I am the true vine, and My Father is the husbandman. Every branch in Me that beareth not fruit He taketh away: and every [branch] that beareth fruit, He purgeth it, that it may bring forth more fruit.

He is the vine and we are the branches. If a branch does not bear fruit it is "taken away." This phrase has also been translated as "cuts off," "cuts away," and "removes;" interestingly, these are especially poor translations.

The Greek word for this phrase is "airo;" the Hebrew word is "nasa." Nasa and airo involve being lifted up to a place of pardon and forgiveness. Christ has paid the full price for our sin; He has bore our sin and removed its penalty from us. He has more than made up for our sin; and in doing so, He pardoned and forgave us. Nasa represents ease. The Word is our place of repose, our place of rest or ease. The Word furnishes us with everything we need and we can rest in that. Nasa also means to marry – to connect yourself to Christ.

When we are not bearing fruit we need to be reminded of who we are! A branch that does not bear fruit is not taken away or taken out of the picture; it is lifted up; it is taken out of the dirt. By understanding who we are in Christ and by understanding what He did for us, we escape the flesh – we lose the old life and gain the new life of bearing Spiritual fruit!

If we are not abiding in Him and what He has accomplished for us we are *like* a branch that is useless. Those branches are burned up - just like the works we produce when we are not abiding in Christ! We can produce fruit that is no different from the unsaved when we are not resting in who we are in Christ. We must understand what He has done for us and we must rest in that! A fruit-producing vine needs to be in its rightful place – it needs to be lifted up. We need to be lifted up, too – we need to take our place seated in Christ!

I WILL- by Kathleen Higham

I will not weep
Or stir my heart to woe
Nor open up the flood
That allows the tears to flow.

I will not grow faint
Or bear a soul bereft
Nor grieve for a moment
That my God has left.

I will not murmur
Or wallow in the night
Nor bemoan the circumstance
That has become my plight.

I will not lose hope
Or shudder in fear
Nor burden the thought
That God would leave me here.

I will not surrender
Or walk with the lost
Nor forget, no not ever
That Jesus paid the cost!

I will not despair
Or question His will
Nor worry the matter
That God loves me still.

I will not forget
Or neglect to pray
Nor hold back my praise
That God deserves today.

I will not be crushed
Or sorrow in my sleep
Nor fail to remember
That I am His to keep.

I will cry out in faith
I will wait and be still
I will trust in Him alone
My Lord, my God---I will...

Day 41
GUILT RIDDEN? – by Stephanie White

Psalm 34:22 AMP
The Lord redeems the lives of His servants, and none of those who take refuge and trust in Him shall be condemned or held guilty.

The answer to the guilt problem many Christians experience is where they are living and who they are trusting in. In the above verse we find that NO ONE who takes refuge in the Lord and NO ONE who trusts in Him will be condemned or held guilty! Too many times we are not taking refuge in the Lord.

To take refuge in the Lord means to place yourself in an inaccessible place. The Bible tells us that we are "hidden" in Christ. We are inaccessible; we are protected, we are covered, and we are shielded! When God looks at us He sees Jesus. If we take refuge in Christ we understand that we are hidden in Christ and we are not going to God based on ourselves but instead we are going to God based on Jesus Christ and all that He has accomplished for us. We must understand what Jesus Christ really did for us!

Do we truly understand that we have been absolved or forgiven of all guilt as far as God is concerned? If God looks at us this way why do we choose to see ourselves any other way?

Too many times we are not trusting in the Lord! There are too many of us who are trusting in ourselves. We do not think we are trusting in ourselves, but when we count on the "good" things we do to "earn" things from God, we *are* trusting in ourselves! When we are trusting in ourselves we will inevitably fail and guilt ensues.

Getting rid of the guilt and condemnation in your life will only be done one way – by taking the focus off of you and placing it on Jesus Christ! Guilt is of the flesh and you only overcome the flesh by the Spirit. Abide in the Word; focus on who you are because of Christ. You are redeemed! See yourself in Christ and get rid of the guilt and condemnation!

ON EAGLE'S WINGS- by Kathleen Higham

Rising oh so high
I hear the angels sing
The softest feathers comfort me
Nestled on the eagle's wing.

A peace that I have never known
When to the heavens, I see
My Father smiling down so sweet
As He reaches out for me.

The eagle sets me gently down
In my Father's arms, I cry
His tears will wash away my pain
His heart brings forth a sigh.

The eagle looks to his Master
Then gracefully flies away
Another soul waits unbeknown
To meet the Lord this day.

Rising oh so high
Through the clouds, a thunder
My heart cries out to be with Him
How long must I wait and wonder?

The eagle has become my friend
He tips his wings to say:
"I am watching over you"
Then blessed me on my way.

When it is time, he'll come
But not to say hello
Swooping down, he lifts me up
To my Savior I will go.

Rising up on eagle's wings
No longer weary shall I roam
Soaring, soaring through the sky
The eagle takes me home...

PRAYER MEETS THE ENEMY'S THREATS- by Stephanie White

Nehemiah 4:8-9 NIV
They all plotted together to come and fight against Jerusalem and stir up trouble against it. But we prayed to our God and posted a guard day and night to meet this threat.

The Jews were beginning to rebuild the walls that surrounded their city and not everyone was pleased with this. The walls represented their security and strength and not everyone is in favor of others being blessed. You may be experiencing God's blessings and man's jealousy simultaneously, but you must understand that God is in favor of your blessing and it does not matter if man is not.

The Jews knew that God was in favor of their blessings. That is why they met the enemy's threat with prayer. They went straight to God when the enemy tried to intimidate them. We need to do the same. Prayer is a powerful weapon against the enemy's plan. Too many times we overlook prayer or we offer the insincere, perfunctory prayer because we think that is what we should do or what is expected. Prayer is a privilege; it is not a chore or a duty.

> Psalm 50:15 NIV ...call upon Me in the day of trouble; I will deliver you, and you will honor Me.

Instead of trying to oppose the enemy in our own strength, we need to go to God.

They prayed and they posted a guard day and night. We need to be on guard in our own lives, as well. How do we do this? We do this by abiding in the Word of God. We keep ourselves out of trouble and we keep ourselves in a place of protection when we continue in the Word. Call upon the Lord when the enemy approaches; cry out to Him for the help you need. He will help you and you will give Him all the glory!

IT- by Kathleen Higham

My heart is weak with pride
About the way I sin
Some things I just couldn't do
No--I would not let it in.

Now age has taken its toll
For the sins that made me cry
And the biggest sin of all
Was the arrogance of that lie.

Discovering that I am capable
Of everything under the sun
No wonder it has broken me
Knowing all the sins I've done.

It is so hard to acknowledge
From it I should have run
If only I could forget it
But no—not this one.

It has surely earned its name
That separates from the rest
And it will wait forever
Then bring the ugliest test.

It is always ready
For the circumstance to come
A weary heart betrays
When stunned we succumb.

Oh Lord You are so merciful
When we are lulled to commit
But Jesus carried it on the cross
And saved us all from "IT."

Proverbs 17:27 NIV
A man of knowledge uses words with restraint, and a man
of understanding is even-tempered.

A man who has knowledge is a man who is diligent with the Word of God. Our knowledge finds its origin in the Word of God alone. Any information we have that does not agree with the Word of God is simply counterfeit knowledge; it is the lack of knowledge.

Proof of this knowledge is restraint with our words. When we fill ourselves with the Word of God it has a filtering affect on our speech. The Bible tells us that the tongue cannot be controlled by man (James 3:8), but we also know that what is impossible for man *is* possible with God (Luke 18:27). He will control our tongue through His Word. The more we abide in the Word, the more controlled our communications will be.

Our words can hurt others, they can discourage, they can tear down, they can defame, and so on, when we ignore the Word. Our words are very important and we must understand that our words need to be under the control of the Holy Spirit.

Many times we let our words get away from us. We tend to like to hear ourselves talk, but we must appreciate the power our words really have. When we are filling ourselves with the Word of God our words will be limited.

Ephesians 4:29 NIV Do not let any unwholesome talk come out of your mouths, but only what is helpful for building others up according to their needs, that it may benefit those who listen.

Out of the abundance of our heart our mouth will speak (Matthew 12:34), so we must be watchful regarding what we fill our hearts with. When the Word is filling our hearts we will speak only what is helpful and beneficial to others.

Day 46
THIS THOUGHT– by Kathleen Higham

Having felt the joy of life
When laughter filled my ear
Everything seemed so very sweet
I thought the Lord was near.

This thought passed quickly
For the joy had turned to fear
Even when all was frightful
I thought the Lord was near.

Once again I am waiting
What more shall I bear?
Is it joy or fear, I wondered
I thought the Lord was near.

Joy though warm and pleasant
At times remains unclear
Fear dark and heavy, still
I thought the Lord was near.

Joy carries me to the morn
My eyes will seek the mirror
As fear takes a bitter hold
I thought the Lord was near.

Having felt the joy of life
And all that I hold dear
Knowing I was right, when
I thought the Lord was near.

Though joy is the noble one
Fear will not let her be
But the Lord draws ever close
When fear would come to me.

So if I should have to choose
To live with joy or fear
This thought, only this thought
Let me be where He is near.

2 Timothy 1:7
"For God hath not given us the spirit of fear; but of power, and of love, and of sound mind."

Day 47
WATCH AND PRAY– by Stephanie White

Matthew 26:41 NIV
**"Watch and pray so that you will not fall into temptation.
The Spirit is willing, but the body is weak."**

The Word tells us that watching and praying will keep us from falling into temptation.

To watch is to keep awake; it is to be aware of what is going on in your life. It is to be watchful concerning what you are filling yourself with. Watching is vigilance; it is being on guard.

1 Corinthians 16:13 NIV Be on your guard; stand firm in the faith; be men of courage; be strong.

When we are on guard we are standing firm in our faith; we are abiding in the Word of God and we are filling ourselves with that Word to the point that faith is being produced. The Word produces faith, courage, and strength.

Watch and pray; keep your focus on the Word and communicate with God. Let God know how you feel; talk to Him about what you are going through and what you need. Continue to walk in the Spirit; that is where strength lies. Remain focused on Christ no matter what the situation.

Watching and praying will not keep temptation from coming; nevertheless, it will keep you from falling into it.

1 Corinthians 10:13 NIV No temptation has seized you except what is common to man. And God is faithful; He will not let you be tempted beyond what you can bear. But when you are tempted, He will also provide a way out so that you can stand up under it.

Temptations will come, but we do not have to give in to them. Keep focused on Christ; He will keep you from falling.

I hear the rumble in the distance that brings to me the rain. The morning begins with a dreary sky, but God whispers with a sigh. "Well I have certain rights and I believe they have been taken advantage of," I say to Him. Silence prevails, except for the vague thunder that announces the power of His majesty. Loud claps of thunder and pouring rain capture my thoughts once again. I believed I had some rights, especially when I knew that I was right! "Oh precious woman, it matters not. Is this why you fight? Must you have the final word as slumber pulls you into night?" Humility becomes a vision in my mind. A man that died for me for no reason but love was worthy in God's sight when He gave up everything, even His right to be right...

I have given up my right
My right to be right
A peace comes so sweetly
My soul warms in delight.

I have given up my right
My right to be right
An amazing little habit
Drowns me in my fight.

I have given up my right
My right to be right
Only then knowledge comes
A vision of God's light.

I have given up my right
My right to be right
Simplified yet exalted
Filled with power and might.

I have given up my right
When at His feet I reside
Given up my right to be right
As Jesus did the night He died.

Isaiah 54:13
All your sons will be taught by the Lord, and great will be your children's peace.

Job 26:14a NIV
And these are but the outer fringe of His works; how faint the whisper we hear of Him!

God created the planet Earth with beauty and distinction. We can look around and see His power and vision displayed in His creation each and every day. Watching the sun rise and set is a thing of beauty that we cannot even completely understand. We do not understand all of the mysteries of this world we live in – in pride we may like to think we do, but we do not.

What we observe here on Earth is just the "outer fringe of His works!" One day we will see Him in all of His glory; we will witness His completeness and complexity and we will be in unequaled awe. Until then, we have these "whispers" of His greatness. Do not ignore these "whispers!"

Open your eyes to the beauty of nature. Take the time to watch a squirrel playing in the trees. Make time to experience the setting and rising of the sun. Gaze at the stars and see if you can count them. Open your eyes to the beauty of mankind. Pay attention to the loved ones in your life and participate in God's greatness in them. Make the time to meet new people and enjoy the people you already know.

We can learn so much from His creation.

Job 12:7-9 NIV But ask the animals, and they will teach you, or the birds of the air, and they will tell you; or speak to the earth, and it will teach you, or let the fish of the sea inform you. Which of all these does not know that the hand of the LORD has done this?

Are animals more informed about your God than you are? We may only have the outer fringe now, but even the outer fringe is more than we can learn in a lifetime. Open your eyes to the greatness of your God and live in awe of Him!

Day 50
THE STORM- by Kathleen Higham

What is free in my life did not come freely to Christ. The storm
He went through makes my life seem like a spring shower. I am
so thankful when God carries me through the storm.

Relentless are the seas crashing down
Terror comes with a roaring sound
When at last the waters calm
His mercy and peace abound.

Winged creatures soar in the sky
Dip and then glide over a satin sea
A mirror image stunning to my eyes
My heart revels in this mystery.

For no one knows of the storm
It strikes with a fearsome force
So often we are unprepared
Careening helplessly off course.

Patience will survive the storm
That rages through a gentle soul
One who never fears what will be
Knowing God is always in control.

Life is of these various storms
But in between love settled deep
Down, down, anchored to the One
Who promises my heart to keep.

Waters abruptly bursts from within
To this world we are birthed in sin
The first fear is from trembling lips
But the storm has yet to begin.

Storms are with us throughout life
Still, we are anchored ever secure
Remembering the storm that saved
On the Cross He would endure.

Thunder shook the earth that night
From the Heavens it rained His tears
The Father wept, then swept away
Every sin for thousands of years.

My God is waiting in the storm
As it batters me until I see
Then carries me to the One I love
The One Who first loved me.

Day 51
NO MORE PRISON CLOTHES– by Stephanie White

Jeremiah 52:33 NIV
So Jehoiachin put aside his prison clothes and for the rest of his life ate regularly at the king's table.

It is time for Christians to put aside their prison clothes and eat regularly at *the* King's table.

Once we receive Christ as Savior we set out to live life as a Christian. This does not mean that we will no longer struggle or have problems, but it does mean that we can focus on Christ instead of the problems.

Too many times we receive Christ and hold on to our prison clothes. We will walk at liberty if we will let go of the restraints of the flesh. Christians live captive to fear, anger, substances, money, and so much more, when they could be walking in true freedom. We need to let go of the old life in which we were bound by our flesh so that we can walk in the new life that Christ provides.

Putting aside the prison clothes requires eating at the King's table *regularly*. The Word of God is our Spiritual food. The more we take the Word in, the more it comes back out of us in the form of Spiritual actions, words, thoughts, and so on. Our works of the flesh are a result of ignoring the Word of God. We keep ourselves in the prison of our flesh when we disregard the Word and all that it does for us.

Proverbs 19:27 AMP Cease, my son, to hear instruction only to ignore it and stray from the words of knowledge.

Too many times we know what the Word says, but we *stray* from what the Word says. We do not *abide* in the Word; instead, we disregard it. If we want to set aside the prison clothes we are going to have to eat at the King's table *regularly* – we are going to have to *consistently* take in the Word of God!

Dear Friends,

When I was a very young nurse I had a friend who pulled into my driveway one morning, got out of her car and screamed, "My water broke and this baby is coming now!" Let me say that my husband drove our car right down the median strip of Belmont Avenue with the horn blaring! When she planted her feet on the dashboard I thought he would have a heart attack! "Oh no you don't push!" I screamed. We flew into Northside OB parking lot on two wheels and thank God the nurse came running with the wheelchair. Her words, "This one came in on a wing and a prayer, don't worry sweetie we are almost there." I never forgot those words and her daughter came into this world three minutes later, on a wing and a prayer.

It troubles me when I hear another say, "If that person would have had more faith, God would have healed him." This is a very misguided and damaging statement. It can cause Christians to be disheartened and maybe even falter. We have all experienced the loss of a loved one. Does this mean we didn't pray enough? Believe enough? Trust enough? Dear God in heaven how could anyone hold these thoughts in their mind and worse yet express them to one who is grieving? One of the most memorable stories in the Bible is when Jesus raised Lazarus from the dead! But guess what guys? Lazarus still died! He eventually died as we all will. Our bodies were knit together in our mother's womb. God planned it, and He knew us before we were ever born. There is a time for every season; a time to live and a time to die. Well surely believing and asking God for help can bring healing. I believe this is absolutely true, but when God calls you home, it has nothing to do with how strong your faith is. It is simply your appointed time to rejoice with your Father in heaven. I don't know why some join Him at such a young age, but you can be sure that God knows. Someone, somewhere, somehow was touched by God when these sorrows came to be. I know this because I have experienced it firsthand when my mom died. Most of you know that I found her body. She was too young, too wonderful, and too precious to die. It took me one year to accept why; not exactly why, but to find peace. Her death caused me to ask Jesus Christ into my life. Romans 8:28 "All things work together for the good for those who are called according to His purpose." Before my mom died I had no purpose in my life with God, but through this tragic loss came peace, knowledge, and joy. When you find yourself so low, there is only one place to go. I lifted my eyes to God, cried out to Him and mercifully He took me in. My mom died, as a matter of fact my entire family, parents, brothers have all passed away. I see life as a gift, but life with God is indescribable. When I go from here to "There" well, I'll leave my loved ones behind in prayer. A prayer that is answered in God's way. For all of us, all of us will pass away. Thank God it has nothing to do with what we believe. That is the devil's desire to deceive. Our faith is more than a Bible story. It is going to eternal life to live in glory. So, your faith, my faith does not hold us here. It is a Divine appointment when God draws us near. Prayer is truly essential and He loves to hear us pray. But our faith, belief, and prayers, though grand, will not alter the celebration He has planned. It was never about faith or fate. Only God knows the time and date. When at last we see His face, there will be no thought of the previous place. Faith is how we live each day and it pulls us closer when we pray. One more breath He gives to me. Till one day a final sigh, for this old body was meant to die, but the spirit was meant to fly to the heavens on your prayer. On an eagle's wing without a care; to be with God my Father, who waits there...

Feeling a fluttering, warmth
That brings His holy sigh
I am there with my Father
Left behind loved ones to cry.

I rode your prayer to heaven
Please do not wonder why
There is peace, so much peace
It was time for me to die.

Do not ponder your faith
Believing we could rearrange
For my God the Father knows
Some things prayers won't change.

There is a celebration, grand!
The angels are singing my story
I rode your prayer to heaven
To my Father to share His Glory.

Do not ponder your belief
The date was divinely appointed
He waits patiently for each of us
By Him we are all anointed.

Feeling a fluttering, warmth
As His presence fills the air
Riding on an eagle's wing, to
Heaven: On a wing and a prayer.

Proverbs 23:5
"They fly away like an eagle toward heaven."

Exodus 19:4
**"Have you seen what I did to the Egyptians, and how I
bore you on eagle's wings and brought you to Myself."**

Day 53
GOOD GRIEF! - by Stephanie White

1 Peter 1:6-9 NIV
In this you greatly rejoice, though now for a little while
you may have had to suffer grief in all kinds of trials.
These have come so that your faith--of greater worth
than gold, which perishes even though refined by fire--
may be proved genuine and may result in praise, glory
and honor when Jesus Christ is revealed. Though you
have not seen Him, you love Him; and even though you do
not see Him now, you believe in Him and are filled with an
inexpressible and glorious joy...

"Good" grief! Is there such a thing? Yes, there is! The Bible tells us that we may be suffering grief for a little while but the end result will be praise, glory, and honor when Christ is revealed – now *that* is good! If we can look ahead and see the outcome of the trial we can begin to consider the grief "good."

James 1:2 NIV Consider it pure joy, my brothers, whenever you face trials of many kinds.

Consider – regard this trial as pure joy; think about it as nothing but joy. Do not fall for the lie that this trial is here for negative reasons. This will not be easy – actually, it will be impossible – in your flesh, that is! Luke 18:27 tells that what is impossible with man *is* possible with God. In order for you to view your trials as pure joy you are going to have to remain connected to Christ / the Word. You are going to have to be plugged in to the promises of God while you are experiencing the opposite of those promises. The Word is your weapon against the enemy and the enemy is anything contrary to the Word of God. We need to stay focused on the end result of the trial – "praise, glory, and honor when Christ is revealed." Do not let the trial keep you from the promises of God.

Dear Friends,

I want to share with you what God has given to me about this word anticipation, but first let me give you the most amazing Scripture I have ever read. It is Joshua 10:13-14 "So the sun stood still, and the moon stopped, until the nation avenged itself on its enemies." The sun stopped in the middle of the sky and delayed going down for a full day. There has never been a day like it before or since, a day when the Lord listened to man. This is power beyond comprehension. We are living in times of great trials and God may not delay the sunset for us, but He will absolutely hold our heart safely in His hands. I can live with that as I sit and watch the glorious sun set in the sky, then later tonight watch the moon shine for me. I can surely live with that...

This month I have experienced the full meaning of anticipation. These are truly times of struggle. Many of my friends and email acquaintances are being tested by trials of major proportions. The single most anticipated fear is health issues. Nothing will stop you cold in your tracks like a pain of unknown origin, especially when it comes in the middle of the night. There is this frightening vulnerability when pain comes late at night. Darkness and the possibility of not being able to connect with ones trusted physician can cause even the most solid person of faith to succumb to an irrational fear. Fear comes from a lack of knowledge. The unknown can paralyze all reasonable thoughts. This certainly has been a month filled with that kind of fear. Do you think because you are a Christian that you are above fear? When pain comes unexplainable and debilitating, I guarantee you that your mind, heart, soul, and finally your lips will cry out to God. There is a need for clarification, for soothing, for peace, for help, and most of all for answers. So now we wait for answers. It can be a very long night while waiting. I have surely seen the fear, felt the fear, questioned the fear, but the anticipation made me recognize how very little control I have over my life. God is in complete control, and there I sat struggling to let go and let God. I wanted to let go, but my science mind was wide open to every horrifying thought. None of us are exempt from the failure of this body, this house, this temporary shell that we live in. We do indeed live in a shell. We have this mesmerizing body that will never be fully understood. Yet, incredible as it is, this body was never meant to last forever. God can delay the process and even stop the pain, just as He held the sunset and stopped the moon, but someday we can anticipate this glorious date. Our most strived for fate. Anticipate: One extraordinary definition in Webster's—to pay (a debt) before due. Oh, I anticipate that God will keep me functioning for a while. I anticipate that God will fix the broken parts for a while. I anticipate that God will use this body until His purpose is served. So every day, every moment, there is anticipation—a waiting—expectation—Then elation! Not one of us knows the time or circumstance of our fate, but still His promise we anticipate. Joshua 1:3 "I will give you every place where you set your foot." Have you claimed His promise yet? The debt was cancelled before its due. He paid it all for me and you…

So often I will anticipate
Forgetting God's plan for me
There are so many promises
That we all have failed to see.

Everything beyond our mind
That hasn't happened yet
Has been paid in full by Him
Jesus cancelled every debt.

Once again I anticipate
Then embrace anxious fear
Trials may come each morning
But eventually they disappear.

God has chosen the weak
If you listen to His command
The unknown will lose its power
When at last we understand.

Sometimes we will falter
Especially in our demise
The foolish things of the world
Will put to shame the wise.

So hold on to His promise
"I will give you every place
Where you set your foot," He said
But first you must run the race.

For if God can delay the sunset
Hold still the moon in the sky
The world will hold its breath
Then hear His contented sigh.

Can you fill your imagination?
With all of God's creation
The debt was paid before its due
Defining this word--anticipation...

Day 55
POWER-PACKED- by Stephanie White

Isaiah 33:13 NIV
You who are far away, hear what I have done; you who are near, acknowledge My power!

We who are near will acknowledge God's power. What does it mean to be near? It means to be an ally or partner; those who are close are those who are connected with Christ. Their identity is found in Him.

What does it mean to acknowledge?

> ACKNOWLEDGE: to *know* (properly to establish by *seeing*); admit, acquaintance be aware, comprehend, consider, declare, discover, endued with, familiar friend, feel, know, mark, perceive, regard, have respect, teach, (can) tell, understand.

When we are connected with Christ we will know His power; we will see His power at work in our lives because His Word is being established in our lives. As we abide in the Word we become increasingly more aware of His power. The Word produces faith and that faith is power; faith overcomes whatever comes against us (1 John 5:4).

The more we fill ourselves with the Word, the more we have regard and respect for His power. We understand that it is not about us; we realize that we have no power outside of Christ.

Acknowledging His power means that you are familiar with His power; you are friendly with the power of God. You perceive it in your daily life and you declare it to others. You can also teach about His power; you know what the Word proclaims concerning His power. Those who are far away will hear about the power of God through us.

Fill yourself with the Word and declare His power now!

THE PURPOSE OF THE WALK– by Kathleen Higham

Dear Friends,

When the walk becomes the fight, your effectiveness is proportionately related to your belief in the cause. If you do not believe with all your heart that what you are fighting for is true, you will stumble in your walk. I have stumbled, I have crawled, I have fallen, and at some point even sat out for a while. Wanting to walk the walk is not enough. Believing is paramount. When every second of your life there is that doubt, that concern, is this real? Is the walk for God, or is the walk for me? Life will be exhausting if you think the walk is anything about you. So many times we get caught up in our own sorrow, and then the walk becomes painfully slow and arduous. Soon we find ourselves on our knees, no longer participating in the walk. We are at a standstill. An enormous hill is at our feet. The walk has become the fight. Every single day turns into a battle. Do you believe that God does not desire for us to walk the walk in defeat?

Last night my husband and I took a walk. We went to the park, and it was just packed with people. I enjoy watching people. There was no quiet walk that I could see. Brisk, running, and anxious faces pursuing what? The walk? I was so happy to be able to walk with Jim, and I thank God once again for this time we shared. Time can be absolutely inconsequential if your walk is a burden. I would prefer to walk in quiet peace for a short while, than to walk in disappointment for a long while. God has allowed me to see many who do indeed walk without hope, without belief, without truth, and filled with grief. How could I know this? Well, I have walked that walk. Sometimes there was so much anger in me when the walk hurt. This week I have felt the presence of God in my life, my walk, and lastly my talk. Last night I spoke to a woman who was so heartbroken. God revealed to me the purpose of the walk. One must walk the walk of sorrow and learn from it. Here is the lesson and the Scripture. Romans 8:28 "All things work together for the good for those who have been called for His purpose." So on this night my purpose became a Holy stroll, when God brings to me a weary soul. I am in awe of His grace, His mercy, and amazingly, His interest in using me. There is surely nothing I can do but walk. Walk until I spiritually collide. Then the moment of truth will come. He was always walking by my side. Oh, I will walk with those who hurt, then listen as they talk. Now I understand the purpose---the purpose of the walk...

The walk is not the cure
But the reason we would endure
Lifting up a weary soul
The walk becomes a Holy stroll.

I have wondered of the walk
Felt the sorrow and the shock
Stumbled, fell, then stood still
Gazed upon an enormous hill.

The walk was never ever mine
But my Lord gave me a sign
My love is all you really need
Walk with Me and I will lead.

No longer walking on my own
Believing that I was all alone
God had purposed in my life
Carried me through pain and strife.

The walk, the hope for tomorrow
Time with God I shall borrow
Peace comes and soothes a need
Prayers for friends, God will heed.

Thank you for this time, the walk
And every moment we would talk
When at last our hearts collide
He walked always by my side.

I am stunned by His grace
Walked the walk to His pace
Now I run, run the race
At the end, I see His face.

Lord I pray for all my friends
Who cannot seem to make amends
God I pray You walk with them
As You have walked with me, Amen.

Isaiah 40:31
"Those who wait on the Lord shall walk and not faint."

Day 57
AVOIDING EXTREMES- by Stephanie White

Ecclesiastes 7:15-18 NIV
In this meaningless life of mine I have seen both of these:
a righteous man perishing in his righteousness, and a
wicked man living long in his wickedness. Do not be over-
righteous, neither be over-wise-- why destroy yourself?
Do not be over-wicked, and do not be a fool-- why die
before your time? It is good to GRASP THE ONE AND NOT LET
GO OF THE OTHER. The man who fears God will avoid all
extremes.

We can take what Christ has given us and claim it as our own. We can "perish in our righteousness" if we think we are the author (salvation) and / or finisher (daily living) of that righteousness.

Pride is of the flesh – and the flesh is death! We can experience life in the Spirit and then cross over to the flesh by trying to take credit for our Spiritual life.

We can also see our flesh as such a frustration that we just give up and live in its grasp instead of finding the freedom that Christ provides THROUGH HIS WORD.

"Grasp one" – take hold of what Christ is offering; "do not let go of the other" – do not forget who you are apart from Him and do not let your new life in Christ lead you into pride. We cannot be compared to Christ; we have no worth outside of Him; however, we can have our being in Him when we abide in the Word.

When we fear the Lord we avoid the extremes. Fearing the Lord is living in awe of Him. It is understanding who we are because of Him. It is understanding what He has done for us. It is understanding who we would be without Him. We must never forget WHY we are the righteousness of God!

Grasp the new life in Christ and hold on to the fact that you cannot live a Spiritual life without Him!

A MESSAGE IN A SONG---BREAK MY HEART– by Kathleen Higham

Dear Friends,

I don't know what is going on that God would give to me this verse in song. "Break My Heart For What Is Breaking Yours." Yesterday I stood in church and sang this song of praise to God. A startling revelation came in this one verse. I felt the impact of the words and what the worshipper was asking God to do. "Break My Heart For What Is Breaking Yours." Oh Lord, I have been breaking Your heart for some time now. Although I don't know why I have struggled with this gray area of my life, I do know it has been breaking my heart too. You know my prayer and my secret desire. I have asked you for a life not meant to be, and even prayed around a sin that captured me. But, not until this morning did my lonely heart see. Your broken heart desires to set me free. No wonder I am paralyzed in awe. That You would write the words that my eyes saw. Then lift me to the heights that make me soar. Break my heart and fill this page once more. When I embraced the sin that You abhorred. Still, here I am writing for my Lord. The enormity of the truth comes crashing through. How I slipped away then cried to You. Purify my heart and make me new. I confess my prayer amiss. Christians we are not alone in this. Each and every soul that belongs to Him, covets. Covets a dark and hidden sin. I ask dear friends for you to lay it bare. Let God break your heart for the sin that's there. Even now I crave for this one thing, as I raise my hand to God in song. "Break My Heart For What Is breaking Yours." For You, for You my Savior God, I long...

Romans 3:10
"No one is righteous; no not one."

I saw me today; it hurt
Felt the heart of my Lord break
Knowing in absolute wonder why
He did everything for my sake.

I saw me today, ashamed
Coveting a sin I thought hide deep
Crept to the surface of my soul
Still the desire there to keep.

I saw me today, felt cheap
Did I think He wouldn't know?
The gray and ugly smudge was there
My hearts breaks, the sin laid bare.

I saw me today, redeemed
As God's words flowed to the page
The evil one reduced to nothing
Leaves me in his cowardly rage.

I saw me today, revealed
Raised my hands to Him in song
Oh how I have hurt You Lord
Yet, broken, broken for You, I long.

I saw me today, a sinner
Gave my heart to Him to break
But, His heart broke more than mine
He did everything for my sake.

Psalm 52:8 AMP
But I am like a green olive tree in the house of God; I trust in and confidently rely on the loving-kindness and the mercy of God forever and ever.

When we're relying on God's love we are like a green olive tree.

GREEN: flourishing; prosperous; luxuriant.

OLIVE TREE: as yielding, illuminating oil. From a root that means to be prominent, bright – glowing, dazzling (alluring, appealing), and clear.

RELY: to *trust*, be *confident* or *sure:* - be bold (secure), careless (one, woman), put confidence, (make to) hope, make to trust.

We are like an olive tree when we abide in God's house! Abiding in God's house is abiding in His presence or His Word. In His presence we enjoy love, growth, fullness of joy, and every other Spiritual benefit there is!

We are dazzling; we are illuminating oil. We are clear – we are letting others see Christ through us and He is appealing to them when we live in His love.

We are like this olive tree because we rely on God's love. The definition shows us that reliance is trust or confidence. We also see that when we are confident in His love we are secure – we do not doubt our salvation, we do not doubt the Word, and so on.

One definition for rely is "careless." We do not have a care in the world when we are truly trusting in Him – what an awesome concept! The careless one is a woman –relying is feminine – that means that it is fruit producing. Rely on God; continue in His Word and produce fruit!

Day 60
WORTH IT- by Kathleen Higham

Dear Friends,

Yesterday my husband and I took a nice walk in Mill Creek Park. I am so blessed to have this man. We talk about life and his wisdom is far greater than mine. I see the glass half empty, or empty. He sees the empty glass being full of air. I tend to ruminate on hurts that have no answer. He encourages me and talks me through it. Jim keeps everything simple and in its proper perspective. He has had more personal tragedy than any person I know, yet His faith in God is unshakable. God gave us a lovely vision in our beloved park today.

I looked to the woods and said to Jim, "Look, someone put a plastic deer at the edge of their property." Jim looked and said, "No Kath, I think it is real." The deer stood so regal and still. It cannot be real. So I watched for a while. Is this a fake, or is this real? Oh I hate traipsing through the woods unprepared. I have shorts on and low riding socks. There is poison ivy, snakes, spiders, and here I am plunging foolishly in, because that is my nature. It is muddy and there are trees branches everywhere, yet I was drawn to it. As I drew closer the fake deer moved her tail. She was huge and beautiful as she lifted her soulful eyes to me. I took a few not so great pictures as she scrutinized me. It was amazing that there was no fear for either of us. I had a mesmerizing few moments and many thoughts ran through my mind. I love God's creations. Trying to get close to her was not easy by any stretch. It was uncomfortable in fact. I got scratched and dirty. I was anxious about the poison ivy that was just everywhere, but oh my gosh, she was worth it! How many times in life do we feel uncomfortable, anxious, and fearful to step out? The unknown presents many obstacles, yet the gift is so worth it! I have found this to be true in personal relationships with family, friends, and simply people in general. But, it is worth it when the outcome brings joy, love, awe, peace, and deep thoughts of our Lord. There will be times when we take that rugged walk and sadly find the fake. It happens, and it will happen to you. When it does maybe there is a reason. A reason we can't know. God will always bring a message in His time about what is real and what is fake. When we get older and possess wisdom, and I use this term loosely since I have yet to actually own it. We tend to believe we can tell the difference. Here is my quote about life. "Nothing is as it seems." I have always known this, yet I have found myself forgetting this absolute truth more than I care to admit. Well, know this; Only God is real! The things we think are real have the potential to disappoint. Hurtful lessons will bring vague symptoms of wisdom. Some people have short term memory. I have short term wisdom along with short term memory. God gave me a most beautiful vision today of this deer. I found her to be real because I was willing to walk the rugged path just to get close. I can't say she was all that happy to be with me, but she stood her ground and did not bolt. She was so worth it. So here is the lesson. Whatever holds you back, push through it. If it is of God He will take you to it, then through it. I am so glad I took the unpredictable path and met those beautiful, soulful eyes. I wish it was longer. I wish we had more time. We may not always be able to find these moments and get close, but we surely can abide in the joy when God does give us this time, even when the duration is not long lasting. There is a reason that I was drawn to her. Those soulful eyes stopped my heart, and then she darted from me. Quietly I whispered, "Please don't go." But God would let me see. She was worth it, she truly was. The deer just needed to be free...

Of course the passage came to me. Psalm 42 "As the deer pants for the water brooks, so pants my soul for You, O God." I would ask you to take the time to read the entire Psalm.

"The Deer"

As I walked, I spoke to You
Animals scurried all around me
Then suddenly she stepped out
This beautiful deer I see.

And only for that moment
She stood so very still
I held my breath and watched her
As my eyes began to fill.

Only God could make this creature
Her eyes darted everywhere
Standing in awe of her perfection
She knew that I was there.

In my head a psalm appeared
A perfect time to find
The deer pants for the water
And I played it in my mind.

Then gracefully she bolted
As if she ran to You
I pictured the stream flowing
Knowing what the deer would do.

Lowering her head in elegance
The water is fresh and cold
A thirst is satisfied again
As the psalm begins to unfold.

As the deer pants for the water
I thirst inside my soul
Drinking in everlasting life
You complete me, make me whole.

Oh, let me see her one more time
For the deer has become the story
And the striking beauty of her life
To show the world Your Glory.

Day 61
CHEER AND COURAGE- by Stephanie White

2 Chronicles 17:4-6 AMP
But sought and yearned with all his desire for the Lord, the God of his father, and walked in His commandments and not after the ways of Israel. Therefore the Lord established the kingdom in his hand; and all Judah brought tribute to Jehoshaphat, and he had great riches and honor. His heart was cheered and his courage was high in the ways of the Lord; moreover, he took away the high places and the Asherim out of Judah.

Cheer and courage - we need both! To have a heart that is cheered is such a blessing. Nehemiah, chapter eight and verse ten, tells us that joy or cheer is strength. When we are sad or depressed we are weak. This cheer comes to us as we seek and yearn with all of our desire for the Lord. Seeking God requires abiding in His Word. The more we are in the Word of God, the more we will experience a heart full of cheer. Even in the midst of trials we can rejoice when we are full of the Word. The Word of God is *good* news – it keeps us cheerful! It keeps us looking forward to the awesome plans God has for us.

Courage is also the result of seeking God, of abiding in the Word. Courage is confidence; it is faith. As we abide in the Word we will experience faith. The Word produces faith in us and faith is our victory. Faith will overcome anything that is opposing the Word in our lives.

We also see that Jehoshaphat removed the false idols in his kingdom. Deuteronomy, chapter seventeen and verse eighteen, tells us that when a king would take the throne he had to copy the Word of God for himself. The Word of God was to be his focus so that he could rule in a Spiritual manner. The same is true for us. Fill yourself with the Word of God and your heart will be cheered, your courage will be high in the ways of the Lord, and your actions will be Spiritual.

Dear Friends,

Today has been a revelation for me. I cannot recall if ever there has been this much physical pain in my body. It is true that one forgets the pain after recovery is complete. Well not exactly forgets, but maybe moves on. I have had many surgeries and encountered fierce pain, but I was younger and more determined to retrieve my physical life. It seems that pain has been front and center for a very long two weeks. It has not retreated, in fact it has pulled on me, pressed me down, and more than once I felt the desire to just give up. I have aged. It is there in the mirror. Physical pain certainly takes its toll on the body. So now what God? I am like a newborn baby requiring something every four hours. My life is on a schedule now. Even if my memory fails me, my body will not. It screams for a pain pill every four hours. It awakens me from a deep sleep to meet this need. The medication brings some relief, but not before another line is spun like a snake trail around my eyes. They call them crow's feet. A sign of wisdom, or just a release valve that comes and leaves its mark where pain lingers. It is way past the time for this pain to leave, yet it lingers. It drags me to this place and keeps me off balance. I am not going where I want to go. I am so tired. There seems no way to bounce back. I am searching for that firm and immovable secret that the Lord has promised me. Jeremiah 45:5—"I will give you your life to you as a prize in all places, wherever you go." Wow! I forgot about surrendering. I tried to do this on my own. I have pushed and prodded and willed my body to respond. I am so tired of where I am going. To the doctor, to the physical therapist, to the drugstore—This morning when pain intruded, well I finally went to Him. Now this is the secret. "I will give your life to you," He says. It doesn't matter where I go, even into hell, I will come out with my life and nothing can harm it. Because of Him... So now I have the prize. My life surrendered. It doesn't get any simpler than that. Life is the prize, in all places. It is a gift. I am sending Him my thank you note this morning. I am writing of my joy, my peace, my thankfulness for this prize and the places I have been.

My life has been extraordinary. I have stood at that volcano in Iceland. I have walked the hot lava beds of Hawaii. I have hiked the glaciers of Alaska. I have fished the streams of Montana. I have faced the steamy snort of a giant mammoth buffalo. I have swum with ancient sea turtles far out into the sea and was very much alone in that dreamy silent world. I have hiked to the very top of the Haleakala. I have straddled the crevice on a glacier where the bluest waters roared and rushed downward for hundreds of miles. I have walked every step to the top of the Eiffel Tower to look down on the night of beautiful Paris. I have cupped the waters of the river Rhine in my hands. I have heard the soulful and beautiful song of the humpback whale. I have immersed myself in the healing pools of the Blue Lagoon in Reykjavik. I have knelt on the island of Molokai and heard the prayers of the lepers. I have danced the streets of New Orleans. I have jogged the Golden Gate Bridge. I have flown in a helicopter and landed on the ocean's shore. Wait there is more. I have seen the time on the face of Big Ben. I have seen the Mona Lisa through my tears. The greatest artists in the world have stood before me at the Louvre, mesmerized by them, I could not move. I have smiled at the guards at Buckingham Palace. I have walked under the Champs Elysees and imagined war and victory. I have seen the Cliffs of Dover. Yet still there is more. I have birthed a babe and closed the eyes of my mother. I have buried my only brother. But nothing compares to this. On the day that I was born, to my tiny face a Holy breath. Now I am much older, but not forlorn. Because of Him... I was born to a family, poor. Oh, but there is more. Last night I dreamed that I had died, but I awoke so thrilled and cried. Another story comes to tell of my life. The story though it began with thoughts of all my pains. It seems my life in Him remains. I traveled around the world with Him when young in age. He took me to so many places and now they have traveled once again to this page. Because of Him I write through this pain and maybe a little strife; God I thank you for this most amazing life.

"I will give you your life to you as a prize in all places." Because of Him, I have been to all these places then realize, the most wonderful gift of all, The Prize. Because of Him...

Day 63
LIVING MEMORIALS– by Stephanie White

Psalm 92:15 AMP
[They are living memorials] to show that the Lord is upright and faithful to His promises; He is my Rock, and there is no unrighteousness in Him.

Living a blessed life is a testimony to the awesomeness of our God! God tells us that we can be living memorials. What is a memorial? A memorial is something that reminds us of someone or something else. We are to remind others of God and who He is; remind them that God blesses His children.

God is upright – He is just; He is faithful. God does not break His promises. He tells us that all of His promises are "yes" – but they are "yes" *in Christ* (2 Corinthians 1:20). We will not experience God's promises outside of Christ. We are also told that faith and patience bring God's promises about in our lives (Hebrews 6:12). Christ is the Word – we must abide in the Word and we must do so until (patience) faith is produced in our lives if we want to live His promises.

Walking in God's promises is not a testimony to us; it is a demonstration of who God is. We must never take pride in the promises we experience. We are not blessed because of anything we have done – we are blessed because *He* is faithful. We are blessed to show others how good God is.

John 15:8 NIV This is to My Father's glory, that you bear much fruit, showing yourselves to be My disciples.

We are showing off who *God* is. He receives all of the glory when we are blessed! Do not feel embarrassed because you are blessed! Let others know that they can receive, too! Share your faith with them – share the promises of God! They, too, can walk in all that God has to offer *when* they abide in His promises. They can be living memorials, too!

Is there a lake in heaven? Oh yes, it must be true. I've read it in the Scriptures, and He makes all things new. But what about the sea of life? Its beauty is un-denied. Will they live in a heavenly lake, basking at His side? In my mind I conjure this in wonder of the sight. Flying fish that skim the water in absolute perfect flight. A peaceful mammoth whale, dancing on a wave. I see dolphins glistening in perfection. I trust these too He'll save. Is there a lake in heaven? Creatures large and small. Some so tiny in their new abode, in my heart I see them all. Everything they do is planned and perfect in their place. The place where He makes all things new, "The place of the Holy Lake." I picture water no longer blue, surrounded by His light. No sun, no moon, no stars at all, yet brilliant is the night. How can these creatures live and breathe without the salty sea? But God can do anything, and this is what I see. Years and years, and millions of tears; He cupped them in His hands. He saved them for this special place, and He poured them on His land. We will not remember when or why we cried, but the tears that were shed by all mankind are now waters deep and wide. All the creatures living there, they never ever died. For the lake of tears is our long lost past, and free we are at last. Nevermore will a tear drop fall or dry on a sad lonely cheek. We are with
Him in the Promised Land, and the lake of tears we seek. With a golden path around it, and a Hand that's reaching out, with a whisper of His touch. He captures one last final tear, and He loves us oh so much. So perfect are His creatures, and their home is perfect too. Salty tears, in a perfect place, and they came from me and you.

Day 65
LAZY DAYS- by Stephanie White

Proverbs 24:30-31 KJV
I went by the field of the slothful and by the vineyard of the man void of understanding; And, lo, it was all grown over with thorns, [and] nettles had covered the face thereof, and the stone wall thereof was broken down.

The Bible talks extensively about laziness. We are warned in Hebrews, chapter six and verse twelve, not to be lazy because laziness will keep us from the promises of God. This is not simply speaking of a person who never wants to do anything; God is referring to indolence regarding His Word.

In the Word, we can see God referring to us as His garden. We also see the Word of God referred to as the Seed. It is when we are not taking the time to plant the Seed of the Word in our hearts that we are Spiritually lazy.

If we are God's garden and His Word is our Seed, then we must plant the Seed if we want to see a harvest. The same verse in Hebrews that warns of laziness also tells us that faith and patience bring about God's promises. Faith comes from hearing the Word (Romans 10:17); it comes from taking the Word in or planting the Word in our hearts. As we abide in that Word and keep our focus on what God has to say, we develop patience. Patience is a Spiritual fruit; therefore, it is the result of storing up the Word inside of us. Our Spiritual harvest, the fulfillment of God's promises, will only come to pass because we abide in the Word of God.

Along with not being slothful, we must also have understanding. When we study the Hebrew word that was translated as understanding, we see that it has to do with connecting ourselves to Christ. Abide in the Word; continue in it, and as you do, read as the dearly loved child of God that you are! Always look at yourself as who you are in Christ – see yourself based on what He has done for you.

MOMENTS LATER– by Kathleen Higham

Did you ever look out your window and see a dreary,
gloomy day?
Then moments later a rainbow paints the clouds away.

Did you ever water a flower drooping to the floor?
Then moments later see it reaching out for more.

Did you ever say a hurtful word and cause a friend to cry?
Then moments later they hug you with the softest sigh.

Did you ever pass judgment on a sinner like yourself?
Then moments later pull your Bible from the shelf.

Did you ever linger in a sin that causes grief?
Then moments later pray to God to bring relief.

Did you ever experience a terrifying fear?
Then moments later feel the Lord draw you near.

Did you ever have an overwhelming sorrow?
Then moments later reach out to embrace tomorrow.

Well, I have done all of this and more.
Then moments later walked through His open door.

I have written lovely poems while my heart was filled with sin.
Then moments later felt my Lord stir within.

I have felt His hand sift my vilest thought and cast it aside.
Then moments later hope comes, knowing He heard the tears I
cried.

Revelation 3:8
**I know thy works, I have set before thee an open door,
and no man can shut it: for thou hast a little strength,
and hast kept My word and not denied My name.**

Day 67
MINE- by Stephanie White

Isaiah 65:13-14 Ampl.
Therefore thus says the Lord God: Behold, My servants shall eat...behold, My servants shall drink...behold, My servants shall rejoice...Behold, My servants shall sing for joy of heart...

Summer is a time of enjoyment for many, but God wants us to enjoy our lives always. God has many promises for us in His Word and here we find the promises of provision and joy.

As we plant the Seed of the Word of God in our hearts, we can be sure that we will eventually see a harvest. There will be seasons in your life of extreme blessing. God is good to His children! We must recognize the blessings that God gives and never take them for granted. We must remember why we are blessed – it is because we belong to Him!

As a child of God we have a right to all of the blessings of God. We belong to Him and He cares for us!

Do not read God's promises flippantly. They are true and you can experience them! You have the right, as a child of God, to walk in His promises. *You* belong to God and God has good plans for His children.

Do you realize that you belong to God? Do you look at God as the Heavenly Father that He is? Every good father takes care of their children. Why do we think any less about God? Why do we doubt His goodness to us? We doubt because we take our focus off of God and instead we put it on ourselves. We cannot understand why God would want to bless us because we know how undeserving we are, but it is not about us!

God's promises are found *in Christ* – we walk in the promises because of what *Christ* has done for us. We belong to Him and He takes care of His own! Our focus should be on Christ – put it on Christ and enjoy the goodness God imparts to His children!

AN ANGEL SINGS- by Kathleen Higham

How I love to write of angelic things. Now a tender moment carries me to fluttering wings.

It is a windy, dark and dreary morn. The trees begin to bend and sway. Branches are slapping wildly in the wind. No critters venture out to seize the day. This is a perfect time to ponder life and the critters hiding wisely in the maze of woods behind our house. I see nary a bird, a lizard, or even a bug. It seems these creatures of God remain safe and snug. I shall remain as well, protected in my house from the storm that threatens to come. Oh, it surely is a windy, dark, and dreary morn. Yet, much to my delight, I witness an incredible sight. A hummingbird so tiny zips by with wings fluttering rapidly in flight. She flies into the storm in search of sustenance. We have always provided the sweet nectar for our precious guest. Now the most delicate of creatures perches upon the feeder to partake and rest. A miracle of peace forbears the scene. This miniature creature does not preen. Awe comes when the wind surrounds and pounds her little chest. Still, she holds firm in her quest. She is not bothered by the raging wind that keeps others hiding from this display of power that sounds like an angry beast. No! For this tiny one has come in faith and trust to feast. I am incredulous of the strength within this most delicate bird. She flits away as if nothing unusual has occurred. The rain falls in blinding sheets, almost completely obscures my view, but I strain my eyes to see. She comes against the fiercest wind and rain, appearing oblivious to any pain. She comes for sustenance and shares His peace. Now here I sit and contemplate the vision as the world has gone mad and insanity rules, it seems. But, for a God who protects and guards our hearts and all our dreams; for we are not small, nor insignificant. Do not hide away from the looming storms of life that will attack. Fly; fly into the storm fearing naught. He goes before you and prepares the way. Sustenance is waiting in the fierceness of the winds that blow. Fly, fly into the storm and you will know. Be as the hummingbird with strength so bold. Even when the tiniest wings unfold---Convinced that no power, no wind, no storms of life will keep His Word untold. Fly into the storm and soar. Drink the sustenance He gives and far, far more. Observe the power of the vision of this creature He designed to be so small. As rain pours down, wind blows mightily against her breast, yet she chirps to Him a thank you. It was a barely audible sound and I wondered if I truly heard her precious call. Yes, God allowed me to hear the sound of joy and feel His everlasting peace that He longs to give to one and all. The lesson is to know the battle is won. The strength and power is not of massive wealth or size. The strength comes when seen through our own eyes that even the smallest He will use to teach. The storms may battle, but our souls are out of reach. If like the hummingbird you have one goal. Then listen to the sound of fragile wings, and hear the sweetest chirp, when from her heart an angel sings...

Oh, what a dark and dreary day
My pencil has very little to say
But how the poet longs to write
As I see this most amazing sight.

Rain fiercely pours down outside
Yet to the feeder she will glide
A hummingbird so incredibly small
I could scarcely see her at all.

Wind and rain beat upon her breast
Still she perched sweetly in her quest
Not deterred by the fearsome storm
That brutalized her delicate form.

I stared in awe at this little one
Who needed not the warming sun
Feasting from a feeder majestically
Then a whisper of sound, unbelievably.

Almost inaudible the chirp, I heard
Thank you Lord, from the fragile bird
Oh, praise God for her fluttering wings
When from her heart an angel sings...

Day 69
VICTORY IN JESUS– by Stephanie White

Psalm 32:7 (TLB)
You are my hiding place from every storm of life; You even keep me from getting into trouble! You surround me with songs of victory.

What an amazing God we have! He is our refuge in our trials. No matter what comes our way, we have a hiding place. Storms will come, but in Christ we are protected. If we are going through a storm we need to run to the protection of the Word; the Word of God is our place of refuge and strength.

As we abide in the Word faith is produced. This faith will produce Spiritual actions in us and these Spiritual actions keep us from getting into more trouble. The flesh only gives birth to the things of the flesh – if we avoid the Word we will only produce actions that are unspiritual. These actions do nothing but cause more problems for us, but thanks be to God! He gives us His Word and it keeps us from getting into trouble.

We are surrounded with songs of victory when we are abiding in the Word. God promises victory to His children who are walking by faith.

1 John 5:4 NIV For everyone born of God overcomes the world. This is the victory that has overcome the world, even our faith.

What is coming up against you? Anything that this world can throw at you can be overcome through abiding in the Word of God! There is victory in Christ!

As we abide in His Word we can rest assured that we are surrounded with victory. The Word never declares defeat for those who live by faith.

Do not let this world defeat you – abide in the Word and surround yourself with victory. The Word is your key to victory! You *are* victorious in Christ!

Each morning upon awakening before I pray, I wait to see what my Lord will say. This morning He tells me, "I will go absolutely anywhere to heal a broken soul." Oh Lord, I sigh because of You. Some days all I can do is write and pray. Thank you Father, and praise You for the way You care. That You would go absolutely anywhere.

Lord, You know that sometimes I am a coward in disguise when I see hard hearted and mean spirited eyes, I want to speak to them, but simply cannot. I whisper a prayer to You for I cannot go "anywhere" even knowing You are there. It's not that I don't care, or long to share, but this world is now so brutal when Christians speak! So, I write and pray and cry to You for being so weak. Oh Lord, thank You for Your strength and power; no matter where we are, or what the hour, You will come when we cry out to You in dark despair. You will absolutely come--- Anytime, Anyplace, Anywhere…

Oh Lord, is there anywhere?
Anywhere, anywhere, one could hide
That You won't seek and find
Even those weakened with foolish pride.

Oh Lord, is there anywhere?
Anywhere, anywhere, at all
That You simply might not come
And answer their heart breaking call.

Oh Lord, is there anywhere?
Anywhere, anywhere, on this earth
That Your hand won't reach out to touch
For You have moved us to our birth.

Oh Lord, is there anywhere?
Anywhere, anywhere, a place dark and cold
That Your feet shall not carry You
To the hardened heart grown bold.

Oh Lord, is there anywhere?
Anywhere, anywhere, Your love doesn't cherish
That Your perfect Word won't penetrate
You're not willing for any to perish!

Oh Lord, is there anywhere?
Anywhere, anywhere, a soul You would deny
That anytime, anyplace, anywhere, You can't go
Impossible! Impossible! For You can never lie.

Oh Lord, is there anywhere?
Anywhere, anywhere, unreachable thru prayer
That Your mercy isn't absolutely there? Never!
You will come, anytime, anyplace, anywhere...

2 Peter 3:9
The Lord is not slack concerning His promise, as some count slackness, but is longsuffering toward us, not willing that any should perish but that all should come to repentance.

SAFETY AND EASE- by Stephanie White

Proverbs 1:33 NIV
But whoever listens to Me will live in safety and be at ease, without fear of harm.

Those who listen to God enjoy safety and ease. What does it mean to listen to God? The Hebrew word for listen is "shama." When we "shama" the Word this means that we hear the Word, we are diligent with the Word, we gather the Word in our lives, we understand the Word, and we connect with the Word. A life that is lived in the Word of God is a blessed life!

A life of safety and ease is a blessing we *can* walk in.

Too many people feel like a life of ease is elusive; it is intangible. This thought is a lie from the enemy. A life of ease is a blessing that God bestows on His children who abide in His Word. We can live at ease – we can live restful lives – if we will only remain focused on the Word of God.

God promises rest to those who abide in the Word. This is ease. This is safety. A life of rest is a life that is dependent upon Christ alone. We do not have to struggle and work ourselves to death. We can simply abide in the Word, we can live by every word that comes from the mouth of the Lord, and we can enjoy the blessing of God without the exasperation.

God's children also live in safety. We do not have to fear destruction or disaster. We will see hard times in our lives, but we can rest assured knowing that God will work those times out for our good (Romans 8:28). We do not have to live in fear of what may happen; instead, we can live in expectation of the promises of God (Psalm 112:7-8).

We will encounter many opportunities to fear. This world is full of fear-filled people. The media encourages fear, our past can encourage fear, our loved ones can encourage fear, and so on. Even though fear may seem like the natural thing to do, we can live *super*naturally! Faith defeats fear. We can "shama" the Word and watch fear begin to disappear.

Day 72
LIFE IS NOT WHAT IT SEEMS- by Kathleen Higham

If I have learned little in life, one thing I learned for sure. Life is not what it seems. Sometimes life appears to show favoritism to some, allowing them to pass through with little pain and great gain. Sometimes life comes hard and furious, even brutally insane, yet one thing remains the same. No one is exempt from what may come; even if life seems sweeter to some. If I have learned little in life, one thing I learned for sure. If I had not suffered, grieved, and fought to endure, I would have remained lost in my dreams, where life is not what it seems. Oh, if there had been a choice, I would have picked the easier life, but would I understand who God is and how He carried me through every moment of strife? If I have learned little in life, this one thing I learned. When at last we finally see, every heart shall bear His scar. Life may not be what it seems, but only God knows who we are...

Life is not what it seems
But, had I suffered not
Then there would be no knowledge
Of the battle to be fought.

If life carried no burdens
Was always righteous and fair
Simplicity though often a comfort
In actuality is empty and bare.

Still there are those carefree
Who are oblivious to sorrow
Trouble does not seek them
As they dream into tomorrow.

The unexpected has not breeched
Nor crushed their worldly way
Believing they have earned the life
That warms each sunny day.

Oh Lord, hear my cry to You
For the heart that does not bleed
Not knowing the brutality of life
Or the blessing that comes with need.

Need may surely accompany pain
Though grief has avoided some
Even when life looks wonderful
Joy might not always come.

How can one know true joy?
If we live it in our dreams
Without God to guide the heart
Life is not what it seems.

Life is not what it seems
Until we touch the deep
Whether bruised, or not, our hearts
Our hearts are His to keep.

Yet life is not what it seems
Until the Holy Spirit helps us see
Not who we are, but who God is
Hearts scarred with His, now free.

If and when the heart shall bleed
Fear not, for it bears His scar
Life may not be what it seems
But only God knows who we are.

Acts 15:8 (NKJV)
The Word For Today Bible.
"So God, who knows the heart, acknowledged them by giving them the Holy Spirit, just as He did to us."

Day 73
ONE SACRIFICE – by Stephanie White

Hebrews 10:26 KJV
For if we sin willfully after that we have received the knowledge of the truth, there remaineth no more sacrifice for sins.

There is only ONE Sacrifice for our sins - that Sacrifice is Jesus Christ! "If we sin willfully" (or reject Christ's sacrifice) after we receive this knowledge that Christ is the only acceptable Sacrifice, we must understand that there is no other sacrifice. Outside of receiving Christ's sacrifice, there is only judgment for our sins.

Some have taken this verse and taught that we can lose our salvation if we sin after we receive Christ. This is false! We still retain possession of our flesh even after we get saved and our flesh only produces sin. We will sin – and at times, it will even be "willful." David talked about this in the Psalms.

Psalm 19:13 NIV Keep Your servant also from willful sins; may they not rule over me. Then will I be blameless, innocent of great transgression.

David knew that only God could keep him from sin – any kind of sin. He also knew that only God kept Him blameless. Our innocence is found in Him alone. When we believe that we can keep ourselves innocent it is only because we do not understand our desperate need for Christ and we are living in the deceitfulness of self-importance.

If we believe that we can lose our salvation if we sin after we get saved, then we must realize that no one would be saved. Sin is a part of life as long as we have our sinful nature – and we will keep our sinful nature until the day we meet Christ. God does not want sin to keep us from Him; He wants sin to drive us into His open arms of love! When you find yourself in the flesh, quickly get your focus back on Christ!

I AM ASKING– by Kathleen Higham

I was told as a new Christian to ask and you shall receive, to seek and you will find, to pray for healing and you shall be healed. I was stunned breathless with the thought that all I had to do was ask God and He would give to me my request. Well, here we are twelve years later and I can assure you that it is not a simple matter, nor is it a complex matter. Oh, the asking might be simple, but the receiving can come in many unexpected ways. You see, no one can understand the complexity of God's reasoning as He answers a prayer. There have been times when I prayed fervently for many years, until I just quit asking and more or less gave up. There may have been a tiny doubt about this particular Scripture. So, I would ask my pastor or a friend who was studied in God's Word why the prayers so often go unanswered. The explanations have been varied regarding this matter. Some say that the prayers have simply not been answered yet. It is in God's timing, not ours, and He will answer when it is time. I have been told that the condition of the heart and the reason for the request may not be what God has planned for us. Now, I have considered my asking and laughed aloud when I realized the various techniques that I have implemented over the years to hopefully receive the desired result. Of course when the request was answered to my delight in a speedy manner, I was on my knees thanking God. Let me assure you that I was not quite so understanding when my prayers seemed to be floating around in limbo and it felt as if God was not willing to acknowledge my prayer. I have come to the conclusion that I cannot pray my hopes, dreams, and my desires into existence, but I can hope that my God who knows me and all of my desires will answer accordingly for my good. This morning, once again I read the Scripture, Matthew 7:7. "Ask, and it will be given to you; seek, and you will find; knock, and it will be opened to you." My mind begins to categorize all the blessings that God has bestowed upon me in these past twelve years. Some of the blessings were completely unexpected. Yet, I look to God and I say, "I never asked You for this gift and I am surely not worthy, but thank You Lord." The answer to a prayer or a request that appeared elusive and remained in the waiting mode will be shifted to the back burner in order to make way for the most extraordinary unasked for blessing! I wish to reveal that the blessing God so graciously gave to me is writing poetry. It is such a revelation to realize that God knows when to bless, when to send the unexpected, and patiently waits for us to look up to Him and comprehend the gift. His gift is not so much answering in a quick decisive manner, but answering in a slow and teaching manner. I am learning, still asking, and on occasion wondering, "Where did that prayer go?" But, when I look up to Him, my Father comforts me, reassures me, loves me, and then answers at last. He says, "No." "No?" I query. I had completely forgotten that particular request until He answered, "No." Then, I recognized that I did not need or long for what I had fervently prayed for. He knew the request was not what was best. Oh precious Lord, I will keep asking, I will keep waiting, comforted by this: You know what's best. This morning I smile as I look up to You in prayer. Lord, I am asking, asking, asking. I am believing the desired request will be fulfilling. I am asking, Lord. Lovingly He comes to me and says, "Wait, rest, and trust in Me, for I am willing."

So often I find myself asking
In prayer, "Lord can You hear?"
Lord I am asking, asking
Will You take away my fear?

But having read Your Word
Fear is surely not of You
Lord, I am asking, asking
For I fear, sometimes, I do.

Longing, longing for peace
And wisdom to receive
Lord, I am asking, asking
To acknowledge, then believe.

Desiring the gift of patience
Wait, oh, waiting is the key
Lord, I am asking, asking
Still, patience has eluded me.

Understanding, I plead for this
Free of this maddening query
Lord, I am asking, asking
Strengthen a heart so weary.

A blessing unexpected comes
Stuns me in absolute delight
Lord, I am asking, asking
But I did not ask to write.

The answer comes simplistically
A test? No! Yet so fulfilling
My Lord was asking, asking
Wait, trust, rest, "I am willing."

Matthew 1:41 (NKJV The Word For Today Bible)
Then Jesus, moved with compassion, stretched out His hand and touched him, and said to him, "I am willing; be cleansed."

Day 75
IRON SHARPENS IRON- by Stephanie White

Romans 1:11-12 NIV
I long to see you so that I may impart to you some
spiritual gift to make you strong—that is, that you and I
may be mutually encouraged by each other's faith.

Our friends are an important part of our lives. They impact us even when we do not realize that they do. We, on the other hand, also have an effect on others.

Do you long to bless others? Are you mindful of the influence you have on them? Are others better off Spiritually because they are in relationship with you?

As we think on the questions above, we must understand that we are not to be weighed down by these questions. In our Spiritual walk we are only to be concerned with one thing. That one thing is abiding in the Word of God! God's plan for our lives is not meant to be a burden. If we will keep our focus on the Word we will be the kind of friend that has a positive, Spiritual influence on others.

We cannot overlook the impact we have on each other. As we abide in the Word we will begin to find ourselves walking in the blessings of God and we will sequentially be a blessing to others. When we have a problem and we connect with the Word then we will also encourage others to do the same.

Proverbs 27:17 NIV As iron sharpens iron, so one man sharpens another.

God's Word will enable us to sharpen one another. Sharpening is the result of a repetitious action. Our *continual* focus on the Word makes us sharp and it can sharpen others. A piece of metal may be virtually worthless, but if you take that piece of metal and sharpen it, you can have a valuable tool. Your value to others depends on your intake of the Word and so does their value to you.

TURN AROUND- by Kathleen Higham

If you live on the outer edge of your soul and never experience the deep Spiritual gifts God has prepared for you, then your life will be shallow and inconsequential. Have you ever heard the expression, "Beauty is only skin deep?" I believe this to be true. Depth is crucial because in the depth of our soul lies a beautiful and perfect life with our Lord. In the Spiritual realm we begin to understand sorrow as a means to carry us to a higher level with God. We leave behind despair and learn who we are in Christ as our perceptions of what really matters change. We become serious about our faith and are filled with hope for life eternal in ecstasy with our Savior. In this life we long to be a joy to others which in turn serves God. So, if you would step inside and feel the depth of your life, your burdens will fall away as you walk closer to God. Your steps will lighten and your heart will feel His peace. Then down the path together you walk, on your face tears will be dried as He pulls you through the furrowed ground, and then casts your pain aside.

Open up your eyes to what is hidden deep. A magnificent vision you shall greet. Rolling hills of flowers and grass are now a carpet to your feet. God reveals His heart and you come to understand why He wept. A revelation in your soul divined, as the strength of a sorrowed soul is defined. For our sorrow is His sorrow and together we shall always be. And every promise He will keep, when we walk with Him in the deep. If we trod the trenches for a time, or dive deep into the sea, we hear His voice speak, "Walk, walk, dear one, walk with Me." Down, down it seems we fall, but through it all, He is there. "Walk, walk, walk with Me." Hear His voice fill the air. "No more troubles," you may cry, but His promise, "I'll be there." He pulls you through the furrowed ground, where behind you He planted the seed. Walk, walk, walk, with Him, for He is all you'll ever need!

Someday when your walk is done, you look back through that furrowed ground. Before you lay rivers and valleys, flowers and streams, as mountains rise up when you turn around. Oh, Glory, Glory, Glory, we sing for all that has come to be. Glory, Glory, Glory to God! Turn around, turn around and see...

Turn Around---
Life begins its amazing journey
Into sorrow some are bound
But when the heartache comes
Look to God---Turn around.

Turn Around---
The ground, it may be furrowed
And we know not of the end
Just walk with Him in hope
Hold tight the hand of your Friend.

Turn Around---
Walk, deep, deep into this life
Even when the light fades to dim
Walk that furrowed ground dear one
Believe that you walk with Him.

Turn Around---
For our sorrow is His sorrow
On the furrowed ground we weep
Watering the seeds our Lord will plant
So walk beside Him in the deep.

Turn Around---
See the miracle that followed behind
As you walked on furrowed ground
Rivers and valleys, flowers and streams
Greet your eyes when you turn around.

Turn Around--
Sing Glory, Glory, Glory to God
For this marvel that has come to be
Look to Christ for eternal life in ecstasy
Turn around, Turn around and see.

Isaiah 45:2 2(NKJV)
The Word For Today Bible
"Look to Me and be saved."

Day 77
BEGIN AND END– by Stephanie White

Galatians 3:1-3 NIV
You foolish Galatians! Who has bewitched you? Before your very eyes Jesus Christ was clearly portrayed as crucified. I would like to learn just one thing from you: Did you receive the Spirit by observing the law, or by believing what you heard? Are you so foolish? After beginning with the Spirit, are you now trying to attain your goal by human effort?

Our lives in Christ begin with faith and they must end with faith – and everything in-between must be done by faith.

We begin our lives in Christ by receiving the free gift God has given us. We receive His payment for our sins. We do this by faith – we hear what the Word has to say and faith is produced. That faith then leads to the action of receiving.

How many of us have no problem believing that we are saved by the work Christ has done for us, but when it comes to every-day life we ignore what Christ has done for us. Instead of depending on Christ, we continue to depend on ourselves.

Human effort will never accomplish the Spiritual. We cannot produce Spiritual fruit in our flesh. Our goal should be to mature in Christ and that only happens as we continually focus on the Word of God.

We are foolish when we believe we can do anything Spiritual on our own. One of the definitions of foolish is "sensual;" foolishness is of the flesh. Foolishness is dependence on man rather than on God. We must begin and end focusing on Jesus Christ.

Hebrews 12:2 KJV Looking unto Jesus the author and finisher of [our] faith...

Our Spiritual lives cannot be realized outside of Christ. He authored our faith and He will complete it.

Being in the medical profession, I have witnessed birth and death more than most people. I cannot say that I understand why God allows some to come to Him quickly and without warning, and others to linger. My father died so unexpectedly at a fairly young age, but God did give him the sweet pleasure of being a grandfather before he passed away. My grandfather lived a long and prosperous life. He loved the Lord with all his heart.

I believe the end of life is as the beginning. It is God's first breath that brings us into the world and God's last breath that takes us home. If one lives long enough to be called, "Grand," well then God was more than kind, more than generous in that life He planned.

That life was "Grand."

When thinking of a father
It is just amazing to see
A father's love is never ending
Though gruff, he may be.

Years ago in youthful pride
He stood so strong and tall
Those sturdy hands reaching out
To protect us from the fall.

A thought quite unthinkable
That someday he might leave
Those same hands fold in prayer
Tremble before God, but believe.

Words come harsh and piercing
Maybe fear has pondered death
But God holds time in reverence
He begins and ends each breath.

Long past, God breathed out
The a tiny babe grew into a man
And the man became a father
The first breath was God's plan.

Now the glory of God is coming
As He holds that trembling hand
When God inhales that final breath
From a father He called Grand.

Grandfather can you feel His peace?
As His Spirit breathes in and out
Someday the Lord will speak to you
Grand, Grand, Grand!
That's what your life was about...

LANGUAGE OF THANKS– by Stephanie White

Ephesians 5:19-20 NIV
Speak to one another with psalms, hymns and spiritual songs. Sing and make music in your heart to the Lord, always giving thanks to God the Father for everything, in the name of our Lord Jesus Christ.

Learning a new language can be challenging; however, it is fulfilling. Even more fulfilling is learning to speak in our new Spiritual language of faith and thankfulness.

What language are we partial to? Are we partial to our old language of the flesh? We can complain and express a lack of gratitude. We can speak about the negative instead of the positive. We come by this language of the flesh naturally; we are born with a sinful nature and everything that is not of faith is sin. Our flesh puts the focus on the negative; our flesh is pessimistic and depressing, but we can overcome by faith. Faith destroys complaints; faith is full of thanks.

We can speak in the new language of faith if we will abide in the Word. Jesus told us that out of the abundance of our heart our mouth would speak. What is abundant in your heart? If it is the Word of God, then we will speak accordingly.

Our words impact others. When we speak the Word to others we encourage them Spiritually. We share the good news of the Word with them instead of the discouraging message of the flesh.

Thankfulness is encouraged when we speak the Word. The Word repeatedly reminds us that apart from Christ we can do nothing of Spiritual value. The more we are in agreement with this truth, the more thankful we will be. We recognize the work God is doing in us and we are grateful.

Sing and make music in your heart. Fill yourself with the Word of God and sing a new song in your new language! Express the goodness of God to yourself and others.

Day 80
A BREATH OF JOY- by Kathleen Higham

Dear Friends,

"A breath of joy," she said. My heart is warmed. My mind is stunned. Is it possible to live up to these incredibly sweet words? Sometimes one is not aware of how they stir the air around them. Most of the time I feel like a mini tornado. To bring a breath of joy even once in a lifetime is truly a lovely thought.

Now I am not rambling here. I have been ruminating on these tender hearted words spoken to me. You see twice in my life someone has honored me with this thought. The first time was twenty years ago. I was visiting my friend's elderly father. He was an absolute delight. My friend had asked me to give him a little check-up, to check his vitals, listen to his heart, lungs, etc. Well let me just say that I was the one who got the check-up. The moment we locked eyes, he patted a place on his bed. Of course I sat down beside him and was immediately lost in his voice, his mischievous eyes, but most of all, his joy. Time passed quickly and he was such a blessing to me. He had no complaints and as I was leaving he took my hands and said, "You are like a breath of spring air." I thought those would be once in a lifetime words. Words that brought instant tears, words that gave me a sense of worth, words that stayed with me all these years, words that helped me in my career and my life. Yes, once in a lifetime words; until a few days ago when a precious woman wrote to me. "You bring a breath of fresh joy each time we visit."

Once again I am completely stunned. I see myself as a wispy gust of wind, no longer a mini tornado. Last night I spoke aloud to God saying, "God I want to be a breath of joy to You." There would have been a lengthy conversation, but my husband asked me who I was talking too. I do talk aloud often and hate getting caught, so I just pretended to be asleep.

Now the question was, "Is it possible to live up to these incredibly sweet words?" I don't know, but I do know that God allowed me to impact two people in my lifetime enough to make this astonishing statement. I feel a quiet awe that God would bring this breath of joy to me...

My friend once told me
You know you sigh a lot
Do I, do I really?
No, absolutely not.

But, it was surely true
I am aware of every breath
Lived life to the full
Faced the hand of death.

In the morning hour
My breath awakens me
Maybe slow to respond
But still able to see.

That God stirs my life
His presence fills the air
Breathing in His Holiness
And joy, His joy is there.

Someday I'll breathe my last
Remembering this thought
"A breath of joy," she said
That's what my life brought.

Can it really be possible?
For joy to be breathed?
Then He whispered softly, yes
The moment you first believed.

Day 81
OTHERS– by Stephanie White

1 Peter 4:8-10 NIV
Above all, love each other deeply, because love covers over a multitude of sins. Offer hospitality to one another without grumbling. Each one should use whatever gift he has received to serve others, faithfully administering God's grace in its various forms.

Others – what are we doing for others?

Do we love others? We can know that we love others when we cover their indiscretions rather than expose them. Love will promote privacy because love considers others. We do not want our sins advertised and love enables us to do the same for others. Love understands forgiveness *and* forgetfulness; love does not keep a record of wrongs (1 Corinthians 13:5). We can forgive others and cover their wrongs when we realize that Christ has done the same for us. When we feel like our sins are remembered, we want the sins of others to be remembered as well. The love of God abounds with forgiveness. As we abide in His love we will also abound in forgiveness.

Another facet of love is hospitality. Hospitality is a blessing to others. When we invite them into our homes and our lives we are expressing their worth and value to us. A life that is closed off to others is not a life of love.

Do you enjoy others or do you complain about others? True hospitality is done without complaining. The Word of God flourishing in us will produce cheerful hospitality. Others will feel good in our homes and we will enjoy their company.

Love is a gift from God. Are we using this love gift to serve others? Do we understand how much we are loved by God? Do we remind ourselves of His love daily? Gather verses on God's love for you and remind yourself daily of His love for you. As you do, your love for others will thrive!

The sorrow of the young has touched me on this day. Here is the most heart-wrenching comment made by a sweet young man who has suffered an overwhelming pain.

"I have never felt physical pain stronger than the emotional pain I live with every day."

Some people live long and prosperous lives without experiencing the agonizing pain of losing the best friend you ever had. I don't know why these trials come with devastating horror and unexpectedly to some, while others seem to have a care-free, pleasant life.

For whatever the reason, these words, "I have never felt physical pain stronger than the emotional pain I live with every day," have spoken heavily to my heart and reminded me again of the fragility of life. The unexpected, unexplained, crushing blows of this life weighed me down, until I cried to God; *because* though unexpected trials will come, there is an explanation for those who believe, *1 Peter 4:12 "do not be surprised at the painful trials you are suffering."* Well I have been surprised, shocked, and flat on my face on several occasions, but there was a conclusion that comforted me when I gave up my heart and allowed God to minister to me. My failures ran as deep as the ocean, but my God, well He runs deeper. If I knew when I was a young woman of the heartache that waited for me, maybe I would have reached out, cried out, and surrendered, but *because* God was not the center of my life, great pain held me captive. Oh, my tears came and prayers were frantically spoken during the crisis, but repentance and commitment was not offered up to God. And, even though my Savior stood close, held me up, and breathed a Holy breath that dried the tears on my face, still it took years and years and countless tears, until I could not live one more day without His peace and salvation. Oh, how wonderful it would have been if the revelation came before the trials and loss, and here I am, the same person, but forever changed, *because* when I hurt, when I cry, and expect to die, it is not with despair. *Because, because*, those I love wait for me in God's Mansion. And I plan to meet them there; with the promise of my Father God in Heaven, we shall live without a care…

My heart is aching once again
Remembering the failure to repent
Tears flood these eyes this day
Seeing words written so transparent.

Few shall escape the physical pain
Though the resilient body can endure
But emotional pain lurks, deviously
Can unravel even the most secure.

Wisdom comes with age, they say
Time has no favorites, young or old
If peace has eluded your precious soul
Wisdom neglects the trials untold.

Gut-wrenching pain will surely come
With suffering accompanied by despair
Yet, His love will always comfort
When you call to Him and share.

Christians who love the Father
Can't help but cry the prayer
Surrendering the agony of this life
For life can surely be hard to bear.

Our loved ones living in Heaven
Wait joyfully without a care
Because what God says, He does
So, I plan to meet them there.
Because…

2 Corinthians 4:8-9
**"We are hard pressed on every side, but not crushed,
perplexed, but not in despair; persecuted, but not abandoned,
struck down, but not destroyed."**

1 Chronicle 17:27 (NCV)
You have chosen to bless my family…Lord, You have
blessed my family, so it will always be blessed.

You are blessed in Christ. Your blessings in Christ are eternal. God has chosen to bless you and your family. Will you choose to receive those blessings from Him?

We need to have faith regarding God's promise to bless us. We know that faith comes from hearing the Word. Hearing the Word involves gathering the Word (finding as many verses as you can on God's blessings), taking the Word in, and filling ourselves with that Word habitually. When we live a life that is replete with the Word we will believe that God's plans are to bless us.

The more certain we are of God's plan to bless us, the more we will reject anything that contradicts God's Word. If we are not convinced that we can live a blessed life, then we will accept whatever comes our way. We will not cling to the Word on God's blessings for our lives. We will not fight the good fight of faith. We are told to fight – this means we need to abide in the Word because God's Word is described as our weapon; it is our Spiritual weapon. Without the Word we are powerless and the trials will defeat us. God promises us victory but this victory is realized as we abide in the Word of God. We cannot have victory apart from faith.

We must also understand that our blessings are eternal. We do not have to live in fear of impending bad news or the loss of our blessings. The flesh may try to encourage you to expect the negative but you do not have to! You are a child of God – you are not like the unsaved. Your life does not have to be a roller coaster. You can walk in sustained blessings! We do not have to listen to the world's version of "realistic thinking;" we do not have to view life the way the world does. We can abide in the Word and expect the best!

Day 84
EARLY MORNING– by Kathleen Higham

I find myself reveling in the waking hours of the morning. The sun shines through my window announcing the gift of another day. I did not arise to witness this most magnificent sight; still I received the warmth and light even though I failed to pay homage to the passing of the night. There was a time when I did rise with sleepy eyes to seek this vision. When I was young; when I was young time was not a concern. Time seemed irrelevant and moved slowly to the beating of the drum. Now the beating drum has captured my thoughts. The steady beating drum of my heart and the question: When might the rising sun no longer be a gift to me? So now I am wondering if I should rise up in the early morning of the hour to see the glory and beauty of His power! I thought I would set my alarm and purposely gaze in wonder at the ocean's edge to visualize the glow of light that overwhelms the sight. Well, my intentions were good, but I felt the sun awaken me once again through my window. Still, there is always tonight! I shall gaze at another most exquisite sight. The setting of the sun will acknowledge this wondrous day. It has occurred to me that the young run to the early morning in zealous strides embracing life and thanking God for the beginning of another day. It has also occurred to me that the older folk, well, we are grateful for the end of the day and the setting sun, because we have actually survived this day! The rising and the setting of the sun though significant in our daily walk have come to represent the joy of life and how we respond to every single moment in-between early morning and late evening. I don't remember when the reversal came for me, but my peace does begin each morning whether I witness its arrival, or am awakened by it. My peace follows me every day as my eyes look to the sky. My breath slips from my lips in a heartfelt sigh. I thank God for everything from the beginning to the end. And you have brought it all to mind on this day, I think of you dear friend. The rising sun that holds back and keeps the blazing heat at bay, then releases unfathomable energy to sustain us on this day. Wait, there's more. The setting sun that seems to hiss into the sea as if God Himself reached down and turned out the light;

can we truly comprehend His power and might? So, to you my precious friend who inspired me to write on this day, another year God has given to you. In the early morning hour this is my prayer that many, many years will come to bear. In the early morning hour your lovely eyes will see when a tiny glow breaks through the sky; His hand touches you on this morn as He remembers the day you were born. Unconsciously you hold your breath when He draws near. This gift, this scene you have lived year after year. I wish you happiness and peace and joy in the early hour of the morn---especially on this day, the day that you were born...

> Youth, it will always seek the morn
> Drawn in awe to the rising sun
> Make ready to begin another day
> The work, the cause, not yet done.
>
> The early morning belongs to these
> They stand amazed at the sight
> Knowing God has gifted them again
> Courageously push aside the night.
>
> Whispering another thankful prayer
> A tiny glow begins the morning hour
> When the sun brilliantly lights the sky
> There is no doubt of His mighty power.
>
> Youth, it always seeks the morn
> Cherishing those days now passed
> Slowly, peacefully the sun will set
> Youth though wonderful cannot last.
>
> The early morning may shift in time
> And one day you might watch the sun
> Then follow it lazily, hiss into the sea
> Though your work is still not done.

Our God has gifted you, gifted you
Much more than you could ever see
When the sun sets, I give thanks
For the friend you are to me.

Someday I wish to walk the shore
But in the early morning, I rest
Find me gazing at the setting sun
The time of day I love the best.

Time---Oh you are blessed with time
So, praise Him in the early morn!
God smiled when He gave you more
Remembers the day you were born.

Psalm 113:3
"From the rising of the sun to its going down
The Lord is to be praised."

Psalm 8:2 KJV
Out of the mouth of babes and sucklings hast Thou ordained strength because of Thine enemies, that Thou mightest still the enemy and the avenger.

Strength has been ordained; it has been designed and established to still the enemy. What is strength and how does this strength come out of our mouths?

What we translated as "strength" in English is the Hebrew word "oz." This word is defined as force, security, majesty, and praise. Strength or force comes from our mouth when we praise the Lord. Praise is a mighty force that keeps us safe and secure when the enemy attacks. God designed praise to establish His children. Praise is a Spiritual action so it is the result of remaining in the Word of God.

> Psalm 119:171-172 AMP My lips shall pour forth praise [with thanksgiving and renewed trust] when You teach me Your statutes. My tongue shall sing [praise for the fulfillment] of Your word, for all Your commandments are righteous.

The more we fill ourselves with the Word of God, the more praise will flow from our lips! Praise is not lip service. It is not something we can do in our flesh and expect Spiritual results. Spiritual praise, praise that is the result of an abundance of the Word in us, will still the enemy!

The Hebrew word that "still" was translated from is "shabath." This word describes rest and celebration. We can see victory over the enemy and we can be at rest – we do not have to fear the enemy and live anxious lives. As we fill ourselves with the Word of God, we will experience this life of rest and celebration.

Day 86
ALL THINGS– by Kathleen Higham

John 16:15
"All things that the Father has are Mine. Therefore I said that He will take of Mine and declare it to you."

God, did You really mean all things? Even these things that hurt and complicate, then cause us to wait? God, did You really mean all things?

In these times life is often filled with regret and sorrow. Oh Lord, I apologize, but I wonder of the things of tomorrow. For these things that burden now are so hard to bear. All things are not always good things, but still, I am thankful that You care.

Romans 8:28 "And we know that all things work together for the good of those who love Him, who have been called according to His purpose." So God says He knows ALL things work together for the good! These are two powerful words. "I know." Well God I surely know that You know, but oh so many times I must confess, *I* do not know. On my knees I come to You, for where else can I go? You know what I long to know when understanding "all things" fails. My life seems so incomplete and everything in me pales.

Philippians 2:4 "I can do all things through Christ Jesus who strengthens me." How I desire for this to be so. That once and for all, these things I would know. "Above all things," You say. Lord can You hear me pray? James 1:2 "Count it all joy when you fall into various trials, knowing that the testing of your faith produces patience."

The cost of my natural life is everything. All trials, all joy, all things! Yes, even the worst trials fall into the "all things" category. 1 Peter 4:8 "And above all things, having fervent love for one another, for love covers a multitude of sins." Oh dear God, must we love *all*? For all means especially those who hurt us; Our Savior loved all those who hurt Him, and He became "all things." Spectacularly these words come from Him! Revelation 21:5 "Behold I make all things new."

Now we must wait knowing, 1 Peter 4:7 "But the end of all things is at hand, therefore be serious and watchful in your prayers." Then finally, 2nd Corinthians 9:8 "And God is able to make all grace abound to you, so that in all things at all times, having all you need, you will abound in every good work."

Here I stand on top of the world that stretches out as far as my eyes can see. As I lift my hands to the heavens at last, knowing: You gave "all things" to me...

So often in Your Word I read
Of the many things to come
But it is hard to wait for You
I wonder if joy is only for some.

Others are blessed incredibly
And my life cannot compare
Each day becomes a struggle
For these things that seem unfair.

Your Word echoes once again
Then I realize where I must go
On my knees in thankfulness
Because of these words, "I know."

All things work together for the good
I know, I know what was said
Joy washes over me, when
Spiritual thoughts fill my head.

All things, well it means all things
From everything I've been freed
Abounding in Your grace and love
You have met my every need.

Here I stand on top of the world
Gazing as far as my eyes can see
I lift my hands to the heavens
Knowing, You gave "all things" to me.

Day 87
MERCY MIXED WITH FEAR- by Stephanie White

Jude 1:22-23 NIV
Be merciful to those who doubt; snatch others from the fire and save them; to others show mercy, mixed with fear--hating even the clothing stained by corrupted flesh.

Mercy. What is mercy? Mercy can be defined as "love reaching out to meet a need in spite of the person being helped." Mercy has nothing to do with worthiness; it has to do with love.

If we are walking in the love of God we will be merciful to those who doubt. It is possible to reach a place where you become angry with those who doubt. Why? We should feel sorry for those who do not believe that the Word of God is their life! We should pity them because we remember what it was like to ignore the Word of God. When we forget what it was like we are no longer able to connect with others. In life we are all ministers in one way or another; we need to be able to relate to those we minister to. We need to remember what life was like before Christ, before we viewed His Word as our very life.

We are also commissioned to snatch others from the fire. What is the fire? Fire is often referred to as destruction. The Bible tells us that our works are tested by fire and if they are of the flesh they will be destroyed (1 Corinthians 3:10-14). We need to realize how desperate we are for the Word; we must know that apart from Christ we can do nothing of Spiritual value and we must share this with others.

In our attempt to give others aid, we must remember to keep ourselves in the Word of God. Our first priority must always be the Word! We cannot help another if we are not filling ourselves with the Word. If we believe that we can of ourselves give others the help they need, we will soon find ourselves in a precarious situation. When we take pride in ourselves we will fall.

Dear Friends,

Well, this year has been a little rough for sure. There have been some scary moments.

I have feared for my husband's welfare, and I am thinking I may have peaked God's interest when unbelief came to my door. It has been a long and shaky winter here—but wait, there is more. God has blessed us with a multitude of friends, and I cannot imagine one I would find who would put her life on hold to tend to mine. Her words have touched my heart and brought a flood of tears. She writes, "Kath, I can fly down there right now and bring you and Jim home. Just say the word, and I'll be there." This is just one part of the sweetest emails I have ever received. JoAnne Muransky is a perfect example of a true servant. She does not question God about what, when, how, who, or why. She just says, "I'll be there." JoAnne is beautiful! Actually she is quite stunning, but I was referring to her beautiful heart, her gift from God to serve. We are not the first. There is a long list of people she lovingly tends too. I once wrote a poem for her called, "Imagine."

You see, I can imagine God's face when He looks at her, watches her do His work. JoAnne's life is a reflection of giving, loving, and serving. The last line of the poem reads, "His love reflects all that you hold dear." What does her life hold dear? The Lord, family, friends, love, and this promise, "I'll Be There." You are so beautiful my friend...

You're Beautiful

God sends her, He does
To those in great need
When sorrow sweeps a soul
She answers a desperate plead
You're beautiful, my friend.

This gift given to very few
A heart must surrender to all
Nothing is too much to ask
She comes humbly to God's call
You're beautiful, my friend.

Her voice is gentle, soothing
Stays long into the night
Cries the prayers with you
Then holds you ever so tight
You're beautiful, my friend.

If ever I should need her
And where ever I might be
There is no doubt, no doubt
She will surely come to me
You're beautiful, my friend.

For such a time as this
When life is hard to endure
God spoke her precious name
Then lovingly created her
You're beautiful, my friend.

Now I pray you can imagine
These things my heart can see
When you look into the mirror
Your eyes smile tenderly
You're beautiful, you're beautiful
So beautiful to me.

Jude 1:24-25 NIV
To Him who is able to keep you from falling and to present you before His glorious presence without fault and with great joy to the only God our Savior be glory, majesty, power and authority…

Praise be to God! I am faultless in Christ! I do not have to fear God's anger or judgment! Hallelujah!

There are some Christians who do not believe this is true. Some believe that we do pay for our sins. This way of thinking contradicts Scripture.

Some feel like this message means that God is "soft" on sin. We must remember the price that was paid for our sin! Jesus Christ paid the price in full for the sin of the world. It was no small price and it was not "soft!" God hates sin; He hates it to the degree that He turned His back on His Son. Remind yourself of the price Christ paid when you begin to feel like maybe you need to pay for your sin.

Christ has the power to present me faultless and He has the power to keep me from falling. In the Spiritual realm I am seen as without sin in Christ; in this world I still struggle. This world is not all there is though – I can live a life that is Spiritual, a life of Heaven on Earth, if I keep my eyes on Christ.

Colossians 3:2-4 NIV Set your minds on things above, not on earthly things. For you died, and your life is now hidden with Christ in God. When Christ, who is your life, appears, then you also will appear with Him in glory.

Fill yourself with the Word – that is how you set your mind on things above! Remind yourself of who you are in Christ and walk victoriously in this realm!

Day 90
I CALL IT POWER– by Kathleen Higham

Have you ever really contemplated the elements of power? Wind, flooding rain, fire, earthquake, volcanic eruption, tsunami, and death are potentially at our door. Well death is a certainty for all and not one of us shall leave this world alive, except through the power of God and His gift of eternal life. So, how do we manage to maneuver through this life where power is everywhere?

Have you really thought about power? I mean massive, uncontrollable power?

WIND---I call it wind. Wind is power. It can come unexpectedly or even with foreknowledge, wind whether hurricane or tornadic will devastate everything in its path. We cannot stop it; we cannot alter it, or even prepare for it. We run from it because it will absolutely blow everything apart---WIND.

RAIN---I call it flooding rain. Rain is power. Again we cannot stop it; we cannot alter it, or even prepare for it. When flooding rain comes everything is completely swept away. We run from it because it will drown us in a murky grave---RAIN.

FIRE---I call it fire. Fire is power. We cannot stop it; we cannot alter it, or even prepare for it. We run from it because it will incinerate the flesh and leave our smoking bones behind---FIRE.

EARTHQUAKE---I call it earthquake. Earthquake is power. Magnitude is the word. We cannot stop it; we cannot alter it, or even prepare for it. We run from it in the midst of it, as it strikes without warning. Everything crumbles in its wake---EARTHQUAKE.

VOLCANIC ERUPTION---I call it volcanic eruption. Volcanic eruption is power. We cannot stop it; we cannot alter it, or prepare for it. We run from it as everything in its sight will sear to red hot and melt into a hard, black rock---VOLCANIC ERUPTION.

TSUNAMI---I call it tsunami. Tsunami is power. We cannot stop it; we cannot alter it, or even prepare for it. We run from it because it will wash us away as if we never existed and drag us to the unknown sea--- TSUNAMI.

DEATH---I call it death. Death is power. We cannot stop it; we cannot alter it, or even prepare for it. We run from the unknown power of the end--- DEATH.

GOD---I call Him God. God is POWER. We cannot stop Him; we cannot alter Him, or even prepare for Him. But, we can run to Him; we can run with Him, and we can live with Him FOREVER. Power is---GOD.

God is certainly coming, and there will surely be an end, but He has given us the greatest gift of all. Can you imagine what He would send that is more powerful than wind, rain, fire, earthquake, volcanic eruption, tsunami, and death? We need not run from this, alter this, or even prepare for it. It is greater than any force of nature. Only a loving God, who knows of the end, would mercifully and tenderly send this gift; this gift. I call it FRIEND.

Dear Friends, this is the power that we have been given to make life bearable. Love from friends. I recently read a book that dissected and detailed friendship in such a unique and beautiful way. It brought a deeper meaning of what friendship means to me. If one can write and leave a sublime message that carries through the very last word, then what is penned is worthy to read. So this piece to each of you I send. But Lord I pray from the depth of my soul—to simply be a friend...

More WORDS OF LIFE DEVOTIONALS
by Stephanie White and Kathleen Higham:

Available now!
SUMMER EDITION

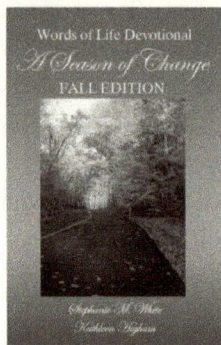

Available now!
FALL EDITION

Each daily devotional is a ninety-day journey through the Word of God.

A SEASON OF GRIEF is a unique devotional designed to help those who have suffered loss and are grieving.

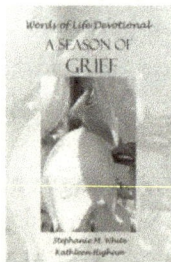

A SEASON OF GRIEF EDITION

For more information or to order more books by Stephanie and Kathleen, please visit us at:

**https://whitestephanie83.wixsite.com/
heavenonearthforyou**

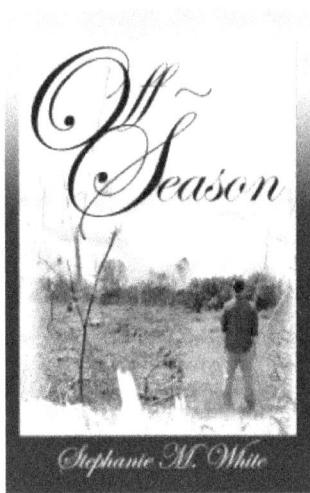

Everyone experiences an off-season in life - sometimes more than one.
An off-season is a dry time; it is a time of lack and a time of trials.

These times can feel daunting and painful; therefore, we must understand the purpose of these times and we must be sure that God has a plan for our good and His glory.

**https://whitestephanie83.wixsite.com/
heavenonearthforyou**

https://www.amazon.com/Stephanie-White/e/B001K86MBC

More books by Stephanie M. White

HEAVEN ON EARTH
REVISED
STEPHANIE M. WHITE

Heaven on Earth: it is a life most people believe is not possible to achieve, but according to God's Word that is exactly what we can have! Heaven on Earth takes you on a journey through the Word of God so that you can find out what is available to you as God's child and you will also discover how to enjoy this life to the fullest.

FAITH IS WORTH FIGHTING FOR
STEPHANIE M. WHITE

In God's Word we discover that we are to live by faith, but we also see that faith is a fight. As a Christian, faith is essential. Eternal value is assigned to our faith. This book is an in-depth study of faith: what faith is, how we obtain it, how it works, what classifies it as genuine, what its benefits are, and more.

The 2 of ME
Stephanie M. White

As Christians, we must understand that we have two natures - our Spiritual nature and our flesh. Each nature wants to dominate, but only one can. This book will take you through a thorough study of your two natures and it will help you understand each one. It will also show you how to rule over your flesh and defeat its power in your life through Jesus Christ.

https://whitestephanie83.wixsite.com/ heavenonearthforyou

https://www.amazon.com/Stephanie-White/e/B001K86MBC

Life Under Divine Influence

God's Truth About Law and Grace

Stephanie M. White

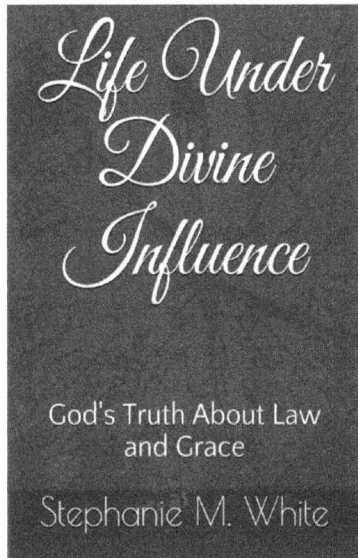

The Christian life is not meant to be complicated.
Jesus Christ came to give us an abundant life, a life full of
Spiritual fruit, a life of freedom and victory.
Unfortunately, religion has infiltrated our lives and it has
robbed us of this gift. We were not created to earn or achieve
from God but we were created to receive from Him and display
His love and goodness in our lives.
We were created to live under His Divine influence and we were
created to walk in His Spirit.
As we begin to learn more about God's plan for our lives, we will
begin to experience the good life God planned for us to live - a
life under His Divine influence.

https://whitestephanie83.wixsite.com/

heavenonearthforyou

More books by Kathleen Higham

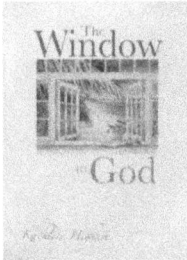

The Window to God is a collection of poetry about the wonderful people that God has brought into my life. Their love has moved me to write poetical thoughts that cross from one heart to another. It is a window to God through which He brings me the story.

Reflections from God is His gift to me; it reflects all I long to be...His. This collection of poetry is a demonstration of the love He has poured out in my life as I rest in Him and wait for Him to move my pen.

This novel is a Christian work composed of truth and fiction that ends with this prayer: Father God, wherever I rest my pencil, I pray Your words will always come. Set Your face before me, when all is said and done...

https://www.amazon.com/Kathleen-Higham/e/B0033RIRJS

www.ingramcontent.com/pod-product-compliance
Lightning Source LLC
Chambersburg PA
CBHW051728040426
42447CB00008B/1026